Macdonald Careers

Television Studio

Judy Lever

Macdonald Educational

Editor Philippa Stewart
Design Chris Steer
Production Philip Hughes
Picture Research Jenny deGex

First published in 1978 by
Macdonald Educational Ltd
Holywell House
Worship Street
London EC2A2EN
ISBN 0 382 06198 5

Published in the United
States by Silver Burdett
Company, Morristown, N.J.
1978 Printing
Library of Congress
Catalog Card No. 78-61232

Contents

One corner of a television studio

'Studio Two is straight ahead of you. Go in if the sign says "Rehearsal".' You leave the receptionist, feeling slightly nervous. It is your first visit to a television studio. The sign does say 'Rehearsal' so you enter. The studio is huge, like a great hall. Most of it is in semi-darkness. But at the far end there is a brilliantly-lit area with people moving about. Making your way to them is difficult, because cables criss-cross the floor like giant snakes.

As you reach the light, you recognize the presenter of a well-known television cookery series. Her face is heavily made up. For the moment she is taking a break, sitting and chatting with the people around.

Behind her you recognize with surprise the kitchen in which she prepares the food. You had always imagined that cameras travelled to her home, to film her in her own kitchen. But here, made out of wood and painted canvas, is the kitchen you had seen on screen—and it has only three sides. Cameras are pointing through where the fourth side should be.

Looking round, you wonder who all the people working here can be. They are very busy. The cameramen are easy to spot. But who is that man struggling with the scenery? Or that girl with the clipboard and stopwatch? And what is that man doing sitting on that crane?

Two things strike you as odd. Firstly, no-one seems to be in charge, though someone must have just told those two cameramen to move their cameras. Secondly, some things happen without anyone doing anything. The lights over the set, for instance, slide to and fro and brighten and dim.

Then you notice that a man fussing around everyone has headphones on. Can that be how instructions arrive? He often looks towards a room high above the studio. It has a glass window behind which you can see figures moving. It is reached by an iron staircase. Slipping away, you carefully climb up and peep in.

Inside, it is like the control room of a space ship. There are numerous television screens with pictures of what is going on below in the studio. To right and left, behind glass walls, are other rooms with more screens and ranks of buttons.

All three rooms have people in. One man keeps speaking into a microphone, others press the buttons. You guess it is from the microphone that instructions reach the headphones. And maybe the buttons work the lamps? If only there were someone to explain everything, you think, and what everyone's job involves . . .

▲ An empty studio being prepared for a programme.

The studio crew

1 Sound technician operating the boom—*see p. 20*
2 Floor manager giving presenter her cue—*see p. 16*
3 Trainee cameraman keeps the camera cable out of the way—*see p. 18*
4 Cameraman composing a 'shot'—*see p. 18*
5 'Props' man—*see p. 16*
6 Call boy, waiting for a convenient break to deliver a message—*see p. 24*
7 'Scenes' man adjusting a piece of scenery—*see p. 10*
8 Trainee cameraman—*see p. 18*
9 Cameraman—*see p. 20*
10 Lighting technician adjusting the angle of an overhead light—*see p. 22*
11 The presenter of the show
12 Sound engineer adjusting sound levels—*see p. 20*
13 Sound supervisor, checking sound quality—*see p. 20*
14 Technical supervisor, checking electrical circuits—*see p. 26*
15 Vision mixer selecting which picture to show—*see p. 26*
16 Director—*see pp. 6, 26*
17 Production assistant timing the programme—*see pp. 6, 26*
18 Producer who helped plan the programme—*see p. 6*
19 Vision controller, checking picture quality—*see p. 26*
20 Lighting director making sure all the lights are correctly positioned—*see p. 22*

Sound control room
Production control room
Vision control room
12
13
14
15
16
17
18
19
20
A piece of scenery like this is called a 'flat'.
10
9
11
8
7
6
2
4
3
5
A monitor screen shows the presenter the pictures the cameras are getting.

In the beginning

The Queen settles more comfortably into her throne and coughs nervously. A cameraman adjusts his shot. A voice calls: 'One minute to go.' Then silence. The programme is about to begin.

Up in the control room, sitting beside the director, the producer feels a sense of excitement. What was just a good idea six months ago is about to become a reality. He thinks back to the day when the idea came to him: a series of half-hour plays on famous episodes from history. The television company likes the idea. He is given an office and a budget.

Having chosen the episodes he wants to use, he commissions writers to turn them into plays. He hires a researcher, too, to check the historical details. Now, which directors should he choose? He knows several who would be good: are they free?

Two months go by. The first script is finished and ready for casting. The producer and director get together: filling all the parts means lots of auditions with maybe hundreds of actors. The director and designer get together to work out the background 'sets'.

Another two months go by. The producer holds a planning meeting with his team to work out the final details for the first programme. The recording date is set and the studio booked.

Suddenly, everybody is busy. The sets are being built and costumes made. Rehearsals have started in a hall near the studio. The production assistant, who helps the director, notes timings for each scene. There are no cameras as yet, so the director positions them in his head, planning each scene shot by shot. Eventually everything is written down in the camera script, which is typed out and distributed.

▲ The director and production assistant go on a 'recce' to a location to check that it is suitable for the programme, and make detailed notes to help them later when filming.

The final day approaches. The production team move into the studio and are joined by the 'crew'. The sets are put up, costumes are fitted and all the furnishings—the 'props'—are in place, down to the last goblet. Now, watching on a monitor, for the first time the director sees how the programme will actually look on the screen. Will the camera positions he has chosen work all right?

As rehearsals continue, the studio 'crew' begin to get the feel of the programme. Their work has just started. The task of the production team, who have been working on it for six months, is almost over. The programme is ready for recording at last.

1 The idea: every programme starts off as somebody's idea

2 Finance: the producer has to work out how much it will cost

3 Discussion: regular meetings are held to sort out problems

▲ A researcher can spend hours on the telephone, persuading people to participate in a programme, finding out details or checking facts.

▶ A production meeting gives the producer a chance to discuss plans for a programme with his team. This way everybody knows what is happening and can talk over any problems that may have arisen.

▼ Some of the stages in the making of a television programme.

4 Rehearsal: actors practise by reading through the script

5 In the studio: the director and cameramen prepare each shot

6 The end result: the finished programme appears on the screen

The programme makers

The planning, scripting and organizing of a programme, the part the audience never sees, takes far longer than the actual process of recording it in the studio. One half-hour programme may take several weeks or months to prepare. A series of programmes can take years. Usually, the same people work together as a team until the programme or series is completed.

Producer

The producer is the head of the production team. He is usually in charge of a series of programmes, which could be anything from a crime series, to a series of documentary programmes with a common theme, or a children's programme that goes out once a week.

This is the top production job in television and most producers have spent many years in television, gaining the experience they need to reach that position.

Very often a programme series is the producer's own idea. He gives the programmes continuity and style, and is responsible for the overall budgeting of the series. He has to be expert in his chosen field. A current affairs producer will have good contacts with politicians and a clear understanding of political trends; the producer of a comedy series will have an eye for spotting a funny script and a feel for what makes an audience laugh.

A producer needs good judgment, because he is expected to act as his own censor and has to decide whether something is suitable for transmission: is this toy safe for children, has that man's opinion been fairly presented? He often picks the team who will work with him too, and has to give them guidance and support to help them interpret ideas and turn them into good programmes.

Director

The director is next in line to the producer. He spans both the planning of a programme, with the production team, and the making of a programme, with the technical staff.

▼ During rehearsal in the studio the producer discusses with the director where to position the cameras.

The director's main concern is with how the programme *looks*. It is his job to turn the written script into pictures. He works closely with the design team, choosing 'sets' and costumes; he selects locations for outside broadcasts or filming, and chooses and rehearses the actors. In the studio he is in charge of the 'crew', the technical team. He decides where to position the cameras, what each 'shot' should look like, and when to cut from one shot to the next. He also has the final word on all the details of lighting and sound.

Directors need a certain amount of technical knowledge in order to know what is possible and how to achieve it. That is why directors have usually spent many years working in television, as editors, floor managers, cameramen or researchers. Some companies run training schemes for directors, others expect them to start directing the moment they are promoted.

Directing can be very hard work, with long hours and a great deal of responsibility. But when a programme comes together well, directing is enormously satisfying.

Writer

Many television programmes use writers, but different types of programmes demand different writing skills. Writing a comedy, for instance, is very different from writing a detective serial. Many serials are written specially for television, as are many plays. Others are adapted from books, by writers who are familiar with the particular needs of television drama.

Some writers spend two years working on episodes of the same series. Others may spend all their time just supplying lists of jokes or funny ideas for different comedy shows. Comedy shows frequently employ six or seven writers for a single programme, and pairs of writers often team up to write long-running situation comedies.

Most writers are 'freelance', working on various projects with different television companies. So they usually work from home or from their own office rather than at the television headquarters. It is very hard to become a writer for television. Although television companies are sent thousands of scripts every year, very few are accepted; and they generally prefer to commission work from writers who are already experienced or well-known. But if you are good, and persistent, you may succeed.

Researcher

People who want to get into television on the production side often start as researchers. They are usually well-educated, often with degrees, and may have special knowledge appropriate to the programme they join. Some come to a television company straight from college; others may have worked as journalists or teachers before making the move into television.

▲ Researchers sometimes have to read through quantities of newspaper cuttings to check their facts.

There is no specific training for them, and researchers' jobs vary from programme to programme. They may have to find people for a current affairs or documentary programme and persuade them to take part; or they may have to travel all over the world, or spend hours in a library checking historical detail. Researchers can spend a lot of their time working alone.

There is no need for a very wide knowledge of television to become a researcher, so it is a good way of learning about television. It is also often a stepping stone to becoming a director or producer.

Production assistant

They often start as secretaries, either in television or outside, and then join a production assistant's training course with one of the television companies. Unlike researchers, production assistants are involved in the technical side of programme making. They work closely with directors both in the planning stages of a programme and when it reaches the studio. They type the camera scripts and distribute them to crews and artists. They draw up lists of all the things the programme needs in the studio—photographs, captions, costumes and props—and look after programme guests, providing rail or plane tickets, booking hotels, or arranging meals and payments.

In the control room, they are responsible for keeping a check on the exact timings of each part of a programme, 'counting down' every scene or item so that everyone knows how much time there is left.

Production assistants work hard, and play an important part in relieving the director of the organizational problems of preparing a programme.

▲ The production assistant keeps a note of accurate timings for every item: in her job a stopwatch is essential. Later her notes will be used as reference to check all the details of the production.

Designing for television

'We need four sets: private eye's office, jeweller's shop, his sitting room, pavement café. By the way, the glass in the jeweller's shop window has to break . . .' The director is going through a script. Beside him the designer makes notes and checks details. What view out of the jeweller's window? Is the private eye's office rundown or glamorous?

The designer goes off to prepare detailed drawings of each set and its exact position in the studio. Television gives him special problems. He has to allow room for the cameras to manoeuvre and has to cope with the position of microphones and lights. Certain colours cannot be used together in case they merge.

When the director has approved the drawings, the designer rushes them over to the scene builders and painters.

A week later he checks progress. The carpenters have nearly finished the private eye's office. It is made of 'flats', wooden frames hinged together to make walls. These have been covered in dingy yellow wallpaper with light switches screwed on. Painters are busy spraying the paper with a film of dark paint. This is known as 'dirtying up', to make the room look lived in. In the far corner, a lamp-post for the street scene is being made from balsa wood. This is often used to make supposedly heavy objects: clever painting ensures they look real.

The designer goes to see the props master, head of the property department, who supplies all the furnishings, with a detailed list: *red* filing cabinets for the office, *extra-tall* parasols, *gold* watches for the shop. The props master has most of them in his storeroom. Others he will have to hire or make.

Soon the day arrives and everything is set up in the studio. The jeweller's shop goes up first. Because it has to break, the glass in the window is in fact made of sugar, which has been melted and shaped into a window pane—it looks rather like a very thin, clear boiled sweet! Behind it, a 'backcloth' is being put up. This is a piece of material, cleverly painted with a realistic 'view' of houses and shops. The designer examines it: yes, with good lighting, that will look real enough. Now, the finishing touches: the shop counter, 'gold' watches (made of paste), a couple of pictures. The designer places them carefully in the set.

Nearby, the pavement café is almost ready. The tables and parasols are in place. A 'scenes' man casually lifts the lamp-post and positions it at the edge of the 'street'. The designer makes his final checks. He is satisfied. So is the director. Nobody would guess that the sets were not the real thing!

▼ The set designer explains to the director and production team his idea for the set. He has made a model out of balsa wood and paper and positioned it on a plan of the studio floor. The director tries to work out whether there is enough room for the actors to move around, and whether the cameras will be able to reach in properly. He also decides what sort of lighting will be needed to create the right mood.

▲ In the foreground is a complete model of a set. Behind it, the actual set is already taking shape. It is built of wood and polystyrene, propped up by wooden beams and painted to look like stone.

▲ Scenic artists put the finishing touches to a set. The 'pipe' in the foreground is a pillar, waiting to be erected.

▲ A 'props' man looks through his store for suitable objects to 'dress' a dining-room set.

▼ Testing time. When a programme is recorded, all the details must be completely convincing.

Preparing a star for the screen

Nobody appears in front of the cameras in a television studio without make-up. That goes for men as well as for women. The studio lights are so bright and hot that they can play strange tricks even with the most beautiful face. So the first stop, before going into the studio, is always the make-up department.

Simple make-up, for a male newsreader for instance, might just involve a little light powder on his face and perhaps some shading to lighten any bags under his eyes. It is much more difficult, however, to turn modern actors into life-like characters from history, or to make a young actor look older, or to turn an ordinary person into a monster for a science-fiction programme. That is where the real skill of make-up comes in.

The basic tools of the make-up artist are brushes, sponges and pencils, and various coloured creams and powders. But to these are added all sorts of substances that can dramatically alter a person's face. This character needs a scar? There is a special substance that can be squeezed onto the skin and then coloured appropriately. That character must have a bigger nose? Wax nose putty or plasticine can be moulded into shape, stuck on and carefully made up to match the rest of the face. 'Fish skin'—a transparent plastic film rather like sellotape—is used to pull skin into different shapes, providing slanty oriental eyes for a mysterious eastern look, or pulling up an ugly double chin.

Make-up can take several hours to do. And, if an actor has to look the same for several days, it will all have to be taken off at the end of each day and done all over again the next!

There are costumes to think of too. What are the characters meant to wear? Which colours go with the set? Does that hat ruin the hairstyle? These are all questions for the wardrobe staff. They may spend several weeks planning the costumes for just one programme, particularly where dozens of different outfits are required.

Sometimes they have to scour through the shops for exactly the right spectacle frames, or spend hours on careful research to make sure the styles are absolutely authentic for a history play. Some costumes can be hired from theatrical agencies, but often they have to be designed specially for the programme. That means a lot of sewing and altering, and several fittings with the actors to make sure everything looks and feels right. It is no use finding out on the day of the programme that the star of the show cannot do up his breeches!

▼ Wigs can make a vital difference to an actor's or actress's appearance, helping them to seem convincing on screen. The hairdressing department keep a large stock of wigs which they restyle for different programmes.

▼ Costumes must fit perfectly. Here the costume designer and her assistant make final adjustments.

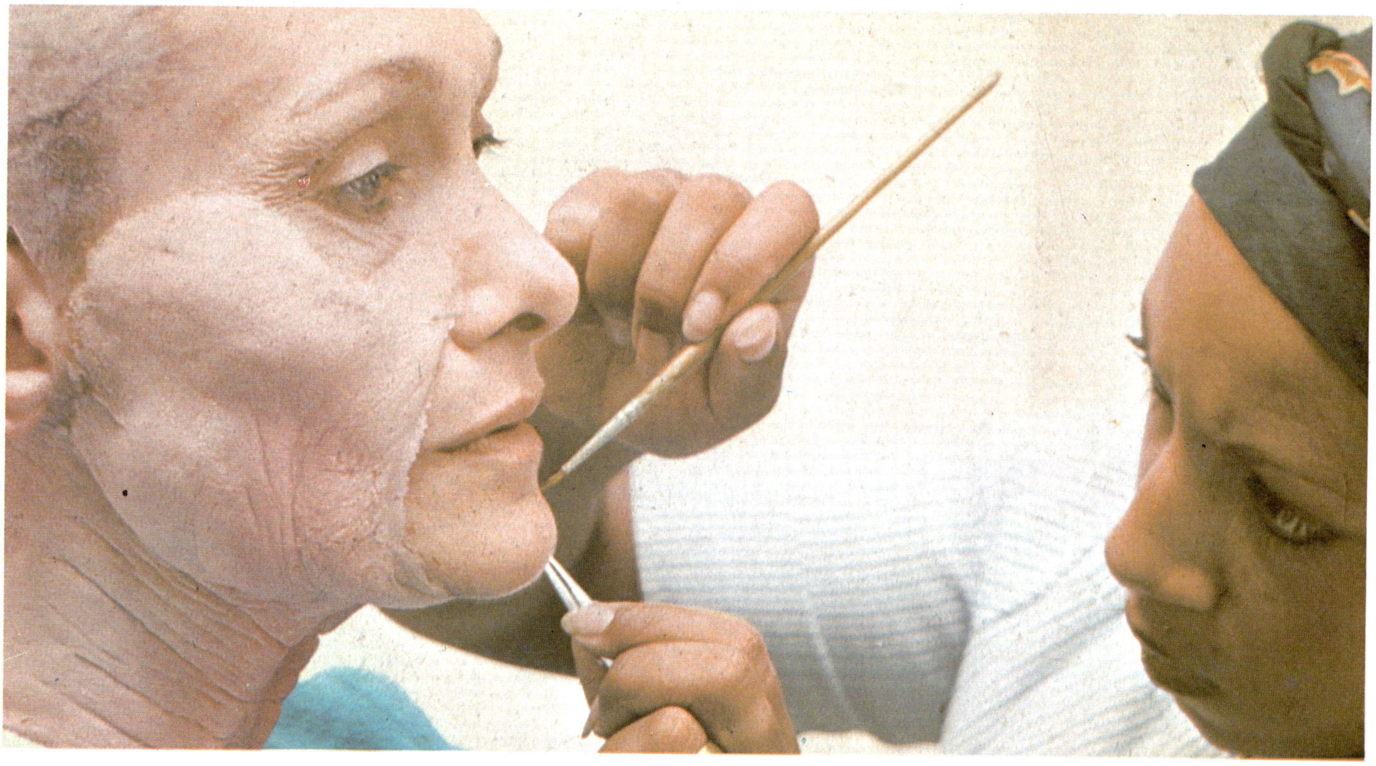

▲ The make-up artist paints a special 'mask' on the actress's face to make her look old and lined.

▼ Fully made up now, the actress looks the part. Her costume has been designed in drab brown to match her mood.

▼ A typical make-up box. These creams and lotions can turn an ordinary person into a vampire, or a tramp.

Contents of the make-up box

1 Different make-up brushes for applying rouge etc.
2 Cleansing lotion
3 Sponges for applying foundation
4 Cotton wool
5 Sticks of cream foundation
6 Loose face powder
7 Palette of eye shadows, liners and face shapers
8 Cotton buds

Weaving the magic

Before a programme reaches the studio, several people play an important part in its preparation. Among them are the set designers, graphic and make-up artists, and wardrobe supervisors. They are all briefed by the director, and then have to use their own initiative to carry out what he has in mind—or often to improve on it. Their special skills can make plays look really convincing, or add glamour and sparkle to variety shows and other types of programme.

Set designer

Set designers work closely with directors to transform ideas into workable sets. They have to have skill in technical drawing and to be good artists: they are expected to prepare complete layouts, position the sets in the studio, and provide detailed drawings of how the finished sets will look. They then have to supervise the building and painting of the sets and choose and arrange all the furnishings. With experience, they develop a thorough knowledge of television's special requirements, like how best to lay out a set for easy camera movement, or what colours and materials are most suitable.

Most designers have been to art school and have some training in interior or theatre design and architectural draughtsmanship. It's important to be at once imaginative and practical in order to design sets that are striking *and* workable.

Graphic artist

Most television programmes include some material produced by the graphic artists—for example, the title at the beginning of a programme, or the 'credits' at the end giving the names of all the people who worked on the programme. These have to be specially produced for each programme.

Any maps or charts in a programme are drawn by the graphic artist, who may have to work very fast to get them ready

▼ The 'scenes' man putting the finishing touches to the brickwork on a painted chimney-piece.

▲ The end of one designer's work!

▼ When designing the credits, the graphic artist has to choose lettering which will suit the programme, whether it is a horror story (*left*), a romance (*centre*), or a pop music programme (*right*).

for a last-minute news item. Some programmes need animated captions; these are like little cartoons, and a lot of skill is required to get the movements of each part exactly right. Some of them are made from bits of cardboard that have to be pulled or turned in the studio. This means the artists have to make sure all the parts work easily, and without any bits of string showing. Imagine the chaos if something broke on screen!

Like set designers, almost all graphic artists have been to art school and have probably taken a special course in graphic design.

Wardrobe supervisor

All the costumes for a programme are chosen and in many cases created by the wardrobe supervisor, who has a number of seamstresses and dressers to help her. If the actors are in ordinary modern clothes, as in a detective story for instance, her job is not too difficult. But if it is a historical series or a science fiction programme, she may have to hire lots of costumes, or plan them herself.

She has to know how to draw up patterns and choose appropriate materials and colours for the costumes. Some fabrics do not look good on televison; certain colours might not suit a particular actress, others might clash with the set. The wardrobe supervisor has to take all this into account as she works. It is then the job of the wardrobe staff to make up the costumes. They measure the actors, cut out and sew the material and make sure the costumes fit well. Just before the programme they check that the costumes are clean and pressed, and that all buttons and bows are securely stitched on.

Sometimes actors need to make a quick change of costume in the middle of a programme and the wardrobe staff have to be on hand to help them, with needle and cotton at the ready in case of last-minute emergencies.

Every wardrobe department has a large storeroom full of clothes used in previous programmes. These may be used again, but often this involves adapting them for the new programme. Here the skill of the wardrobe staff comes in: a change of size and shape, or a new collar or lace edging can make an enormous difference.

Wardrobe supervisors can be either men or women. The main qualification is to be interested in clothes and fashion, and to have a good eye for costume design. Often wardrobe supervisors have studied fashion and design at art college and perhaps spent a while looking after theatre costumes before joining a television company. There they may have to work for some time in the wardrobe department before reaching the top job of supervisor.

▲ Hard at work in the wardrobe room. A major drama series uses hundreds of costumes, many of which have to be specially made for it.

▼ This mask took hours to apply. Now the only way to remove it is in the bath!

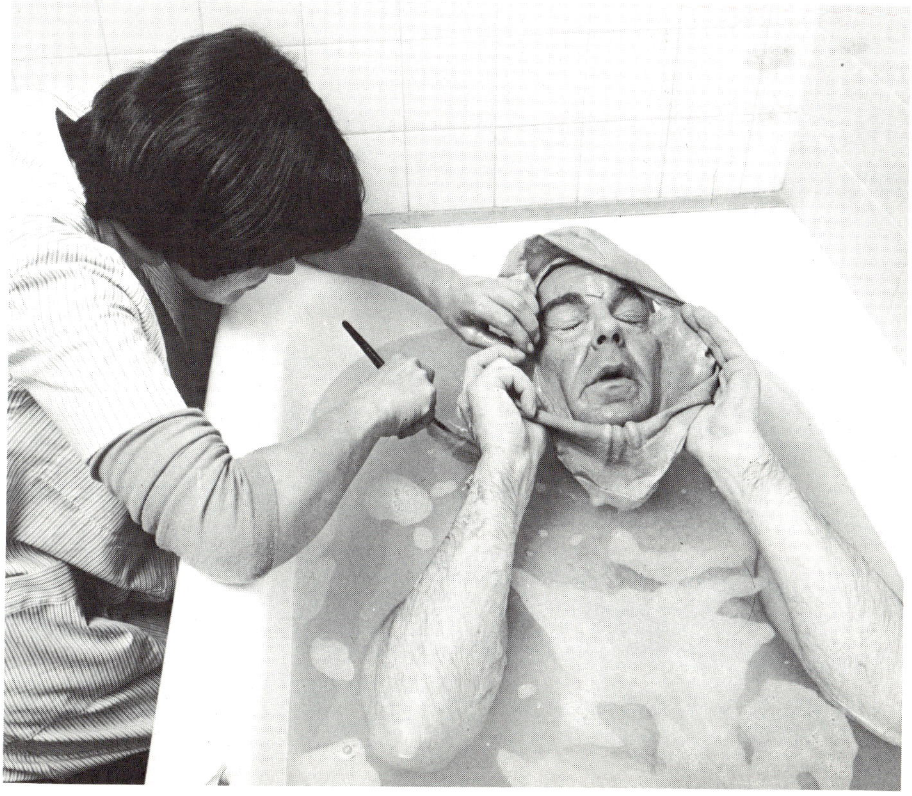

Make-up artist

Make-up artists work closely with the wardrobe staff to make sure the actors and actresses look the part for each programme. Television make-up requires special techniques. They have to know what difference various types of lighting make, how a camera can change the way a face looks, or what makes a false nose look realistic on television.

The make-up department looks after hairdressing too. They may have to design and order wigs for a historical play, or adapt an actor or actress's own hair to suit a particular costume or role. A change of hairstyle can make someone look older, younger or from a different period—hairstyles of even ten years ago are quite different from those of today. This can make all the difference to how believable the characters seem on screen.

Make-up artists need patience; a complicated make-up can take a long time to achieve. They also need tact and an ability to get on well with people: they see actors and presenters at their most vulnerable, just before a programme, and have to be able to chat easily with them to help them relax.

Television companies usually provide special training courses to teach the specific skills of television make-up. But most make-up artists take a beautician or hairdressing course first before joining a television company. Make-up jobs in television are very popular, and competition for them is usually fierce.

Countdown

9.00 a.m. The studio is bare. Cameras and microphones stand silent in a corner. It is dark. Suddenly the studio's huge automatic doors slide open and three men appear, carrying large, brightly coloured pieces of scenery. The day has begun.

Today, a half-hour children's programme is being rehearsed. It will be transmitted this afternoon, 'live', so that viewers at home will see it as it actually happens. There is no second chance if anything goes wrong.

9.30. The designer arrives to check the sets. A real pony is coming and he has had to prepare a 'stable', with fencing and hay. That is going up now on one side of the studio. The 'props' men wheel in a trolley of assorted objects—saddle, blanket, grooming brushes.

10.00. The crew arrive. The cameramen adjust the cameras and check their camera scripts. A voice comes over the microphone, 'Testing, testing . . .' Lights clatter as they are moved into position. The director runs briefly over the contents of the show. There are five different items. He is going to rehearse the most complicated first. 'Set up to rehearse the making-a-chair item,' calls the floor manager. It is his job to ensure that everyone is in the right place at the right time.

11.00. Jan, one of the presenters, takes up her position in front of Camera One. Camera Three is nearby, to get 'close-ups' of her hands as she cuts out, glues and paints the chair. As she rehearses, the director watches the cameramen practising their shots. The production assistant checks timings: every item must run exactly to time.

11.30. Panic! The pony is late. The researcher who arranged the item rushes to a phone to investigate. Another item is rehearsed instead. The 'props' for it are moved around. When it ends, the props men deftly replace everything in its original position.

12.30. Lunch!

13.30. Camera line-up. A final check to make sure that each camera is in perfect working order.

14.30. The pony arrives at last. Swiftly his item is rehearsed. Tension is mounting. There never seems enough time for everything.

15.30. Final run-through. By now everyone is getting the feel of the show. Everything is rehearsed again, this time in the right order.

16.00. A sense of urgency grips the studio. There is only one hour to 'on air'. The presenters go to wardrobe and make-up to get ready. The producer arrives to check that all is well.

16.59. Everyone is ready. In the control room the production assistant checks the time. 'One minute to "on air".' The floor manager signals the studio to 'stand by'. The show is about to begin.

▲ The finishing touches. A table leg is adjusted to make sure it won't wobble at the wrong moment.

▲ During rehearsals the studio floor is marked out with chalk to help the actors know where to move.

◀ Actors trying to memorize their lines.

▶ A rehearsal of a ballroom scene. The studio is quite chilly, and many of the actors are wearing coats over their costumes.

Behind the camera

'Camera One, zoom in please . . . tighter . . . I want a big close-up. Hold it there! Now, move slightly left, can you? Perfect! Camera Two, can you go slightly wider on the two-shot? Right, let's take it from the top again, please.'

The director is talking to the cameramen from the control room. On his monitor screens he can see what each camera is showing, and he is now adjusting them to get the effect he wants. The cameramen hear him on their headphones—'cans' as they are known—and they try the alterations.

What do the director's instructions mean? Let's imagine a scene in a play. The set is a kitchen. Tony and Sarah are sitting at table having breakfast, chatting. Camera One is in position near the front of the set, pointing at Sarah. Camera Two is farther away from the set and can 'see' both the actors.

Camera One has a shot of Sarah from the waist upwards. The director decides he wants to see clearly the expression on Sarah's face, which means showing more of her head and less of her body. So he asks Camera One to go closer—'tighter'—on his framing of the shot. Camera One could move the whole camera on its pedestal but there is not enough room; he is right up against the front of the set. So he uses the 'zoom' lens attached to the camera which automatically makes the subject appear bigger in the picture.

Every type of shot has a name. Camera Two has a 'two-shot', which means literally two people in the picture—in this case both Tony and Sarah. But the director wants to show more of the scene so he asks Camera Two to move back a bit—to 'go wider'—in order to include the table and the kitchen sink in the far corner. That sorted out, the director decides to try the scene again—'Take it from the top.'

A cameraman may be expected to 'frame'—compose—200 or more shots in one programme, and each of these shots has to be perfectly reproduced exactly as rehearsed. To help him he has a 'crib card' which is a typewritten list of his shots, in order. Often he has to move his camera from one part of the studio to another very quickly to frame his next shot while the programme is actually happening. Sometimes the shots are very complicated, like following a dance routine in a variety show, where the cameraman may actually almost dance his camera backwards and forwards as he follows the action.

And all the time there is the possibility that the director will give a new instruction over the 'cans' and expect the cameraman to react right away. So cameramen have to concentrate very hard. Even a half-hour programme can be very tiring.

▲ A cameraman at work. His crib card hangs beside him, giving details of the different shots. Other instructions come through his headphones. He has to be able to react very quickly to get the right shot each time.

▲ A 'wide shot': on the screen we see both the characters, a lot of the background and some of the foreground.

▼ A 'close-up' of the same scene: the face of one actress fills the screen.

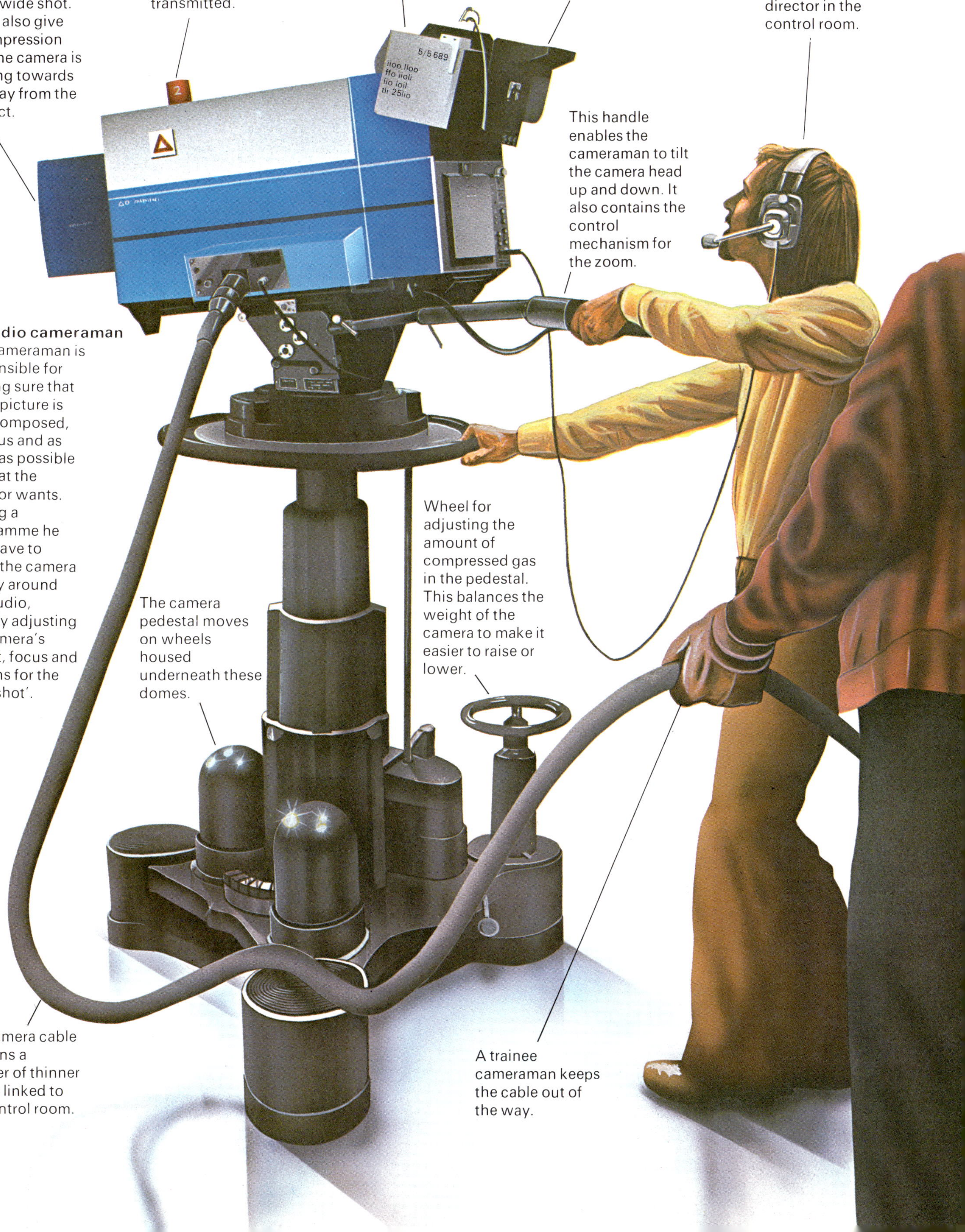

A studio cameraman
The cameraman is responsible for making sure that every picture is well composed, in focus and as close as possible to what the director wants. During a programme he may have to move the camera swiftly around the studio, quickly adjusting the camera's height, focus and the lens for the next 'shot'.

Making sure it sounds right

Unlike children, microphones should be heard but not seen! So you do not often see a microphone in a television programme. But they are there—sometimes as many as 200 for just one programme. Actors and presenters move around the studio and it is not always possible to move the microphone with them or to stop the programme and re-position the microphones. So the sound supervisor plots out beforehand exactly where every microphone should go, and which type of microphone to use to get the best quality.

There are many different sorts of microphone. Sometimes they hang from the studio ceiling, sometimes they are on stands on a desk or on the floor, or are attached to the actor or presenter's clothing. One particularly useful microphone is the 'boom' microphone. This is on a long extending arm attached to a high movable platform. The boom operator sits on the platform, looks out over the cameras and follows the actors' movements by moving the 'boom' from side to side and reaching out over the set just above the actors' heads. The art is to keep the microphone as near as possible to the actors *but* without ever appearing in shot.

Up in the sound control box just above the studio the sound balancer has a battery of knobs and dials on his console with which he can adjust the quality of the sound coming from the studio microphones. Here he can also 'mix in' extra sounds. The director might, for example, want to add exciting music to build up suspense, or eerie music to make your flesh creep. Or a scene might be 'set' at the seaside: the sound balancer can add the sound of waves splashing against rocks, or of children playing in the sea. Most television companies have special effects 'libraries' where almost every sound—from horses galloping or different types of birdsong to the roar of thunder—is stored on tape or disc to be used as necessary.

All these effects have to be perfectly 'balanced' with the studio sound so that they fit naturally into the programme. And each studio microphone has to be balanced, so that the sound is even: if there is a band in the studio, for instance, it is important that all the instruments are clearly audible. There is also the problem of making sure that voices in the studio sound 'real'. It would seem very odd if people who appeared in close-up on the screen sounded a long way away, or if their voices echoed as if they were in an empty auditorium when they are supposed to be in a cosy kitchen. Getting this absolutely right is part of the skill of good sound recording.

Some typical microphones

1 Small 'boom', a movable platform.
2 Ribbon microphone which can be suspended on the 'boom' arm.
3 Very small microphone, often clipped to a collar or tie.
4 Polydirectional microphone (can pick up sounds from different directions); good for recording music.
5 Lightweight microphone, hand-held for interviews outdoors.
6 Similar to **5**, but often used on a stand in the studio.

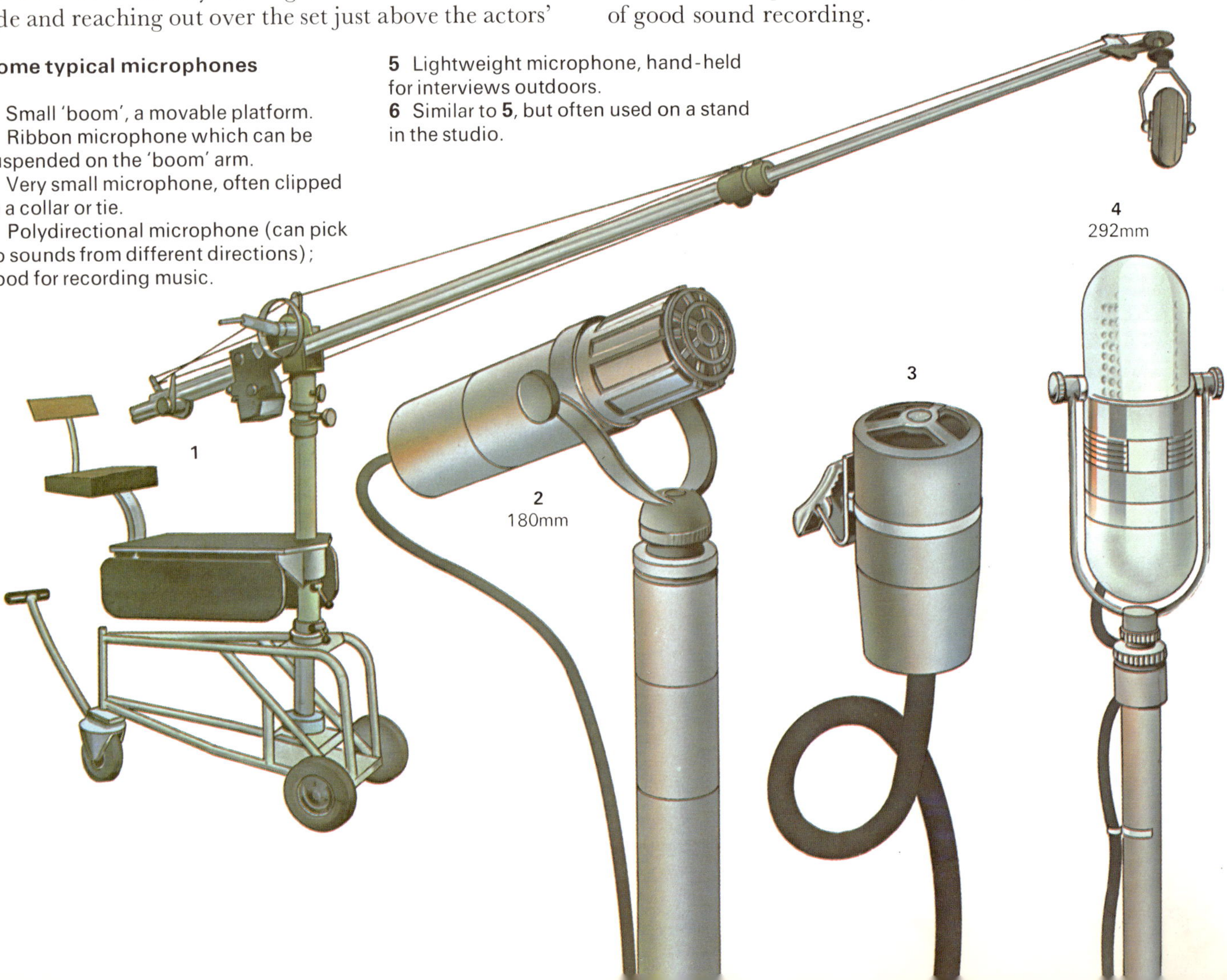

▲ The special effects library. Each can contains sound tapes with different effects, from the buzz of a bee to a volcano.

▲ The 'boom' used to record sound in the studio. Special knobs enable the operator to extend or retract the arm, or twist the microphone itself.

▼ Recording sound for a film. The microphone at the end of the pole picks up the clatter of the horses' hooves, and the cries of the man leading it.

▲ In the sound control room the sound engineer makes sure the quality and level of the sound is right. His assistant, at the top, prepares a special effect.

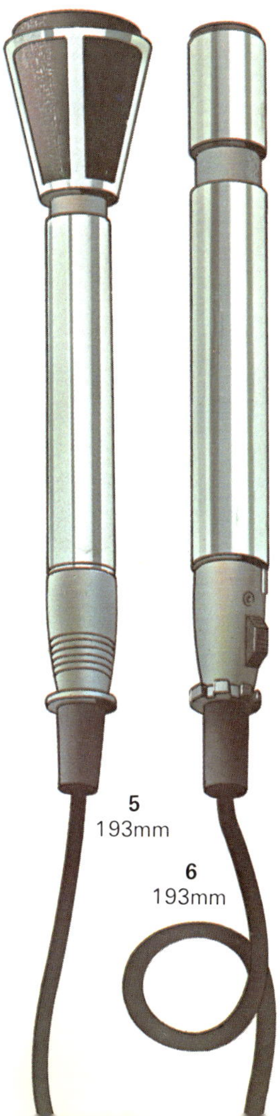

Lighting the studio

Look up as you enter a television studio and you will notice rows and rows of lights of all different shapes and sizes. An average studio contains about 250 lights, and a really large studio could have as many as 500.

Lighting a set is surprisingly difficult. It is not simply a question of turning a switch. Lights create an enormous number of different effects, and good lighting can add a great deal to the atmosphere of a programme. Just think of the difference between a scene in daylight and one in semi-darkness.

All the studio lights are under the control of the lighting director, who is responsible for deciding exactly how to use them. He talks to the director of the programme about each scene and then draws up a lighting 'plot'. This is a large chart on which he first marks the position of all the cameras, microphones and actors. Then, in a different colour, he works out where to put his lights and which ones to use. This gives him a guide for when he finally lights the studio itself.

Now the lighting director checks his plot. Has he got the balance of light right on the actors' faces? Is the villain's face lit just as he wants it, looking sinister, half in darkness? Does the 'sunlight' look realistic on camera? He notices that a microphone is casting a shadow across the floor. Can it be moved or must he adjust his lights?

Once the programme starts, the lights have to be switched on and off at exactly the right moment for each scene. The sunlit room, for instance, may be used for a night-time scene later on. In some studios, the lighting assistant follows the plot for every scene and presses the appropriate buttons when necessary; in many modern studios, however, there is now a computer that does it all for him. The lighting director simply programmes the computer with all the plots for each scene and the computer takes care of the rest.

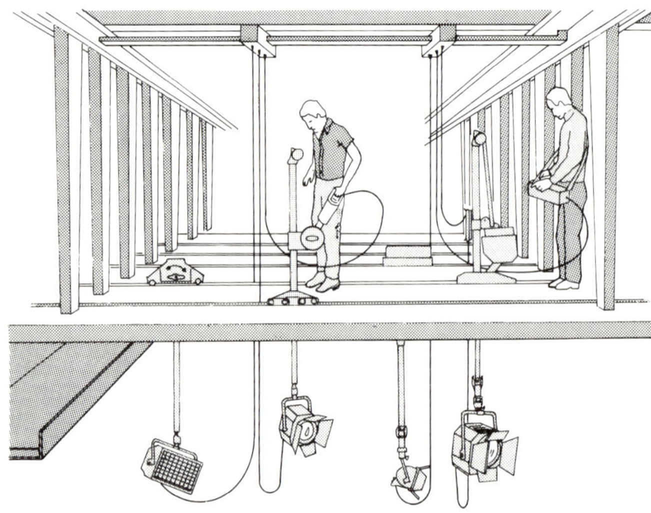

▲ A lighting grid, fitted into the roof of the studio. The electricians can walk on the grid to reach and adjust the lights.

◀ Clever positioning of the lights in the studio gives the impression of sunlight streaming through the 'window'.

▲ A portable computerized lighting console. The computer remembers which lights have to be used and switches them on and off at exactly the right time.

▶ An array of coloured lights in the studio give a discotheque atmosphere to a pop music programme.

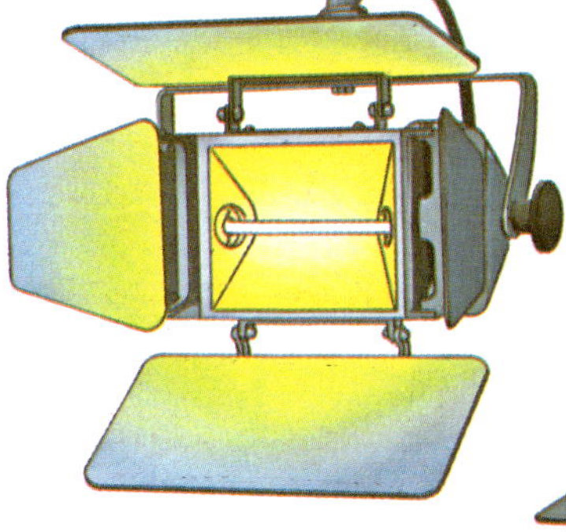

A small, one kilowatt light, sometimes called a 'Valentine'. This is used as a soft 'filler' light.

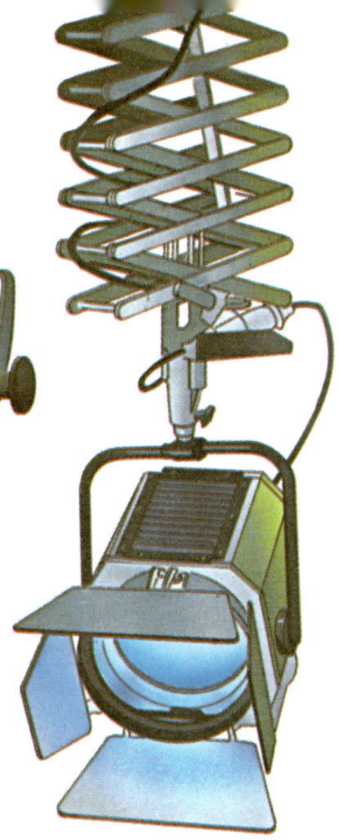

A small spot-light, called a 'pup', suspended on a pantograph.

This has criss-cross arms that can be adjusted for height.

A 'CSI', often used in pairs or fours to give a strong bright light.

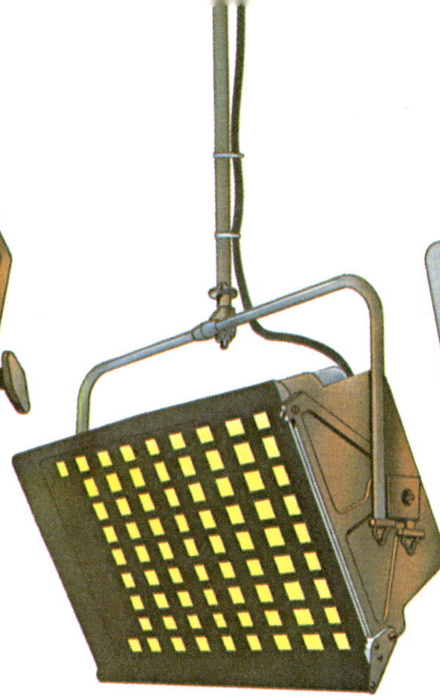

A very soft 'filler' light which can be covered by an 'eggcrate' to limit the light spread.

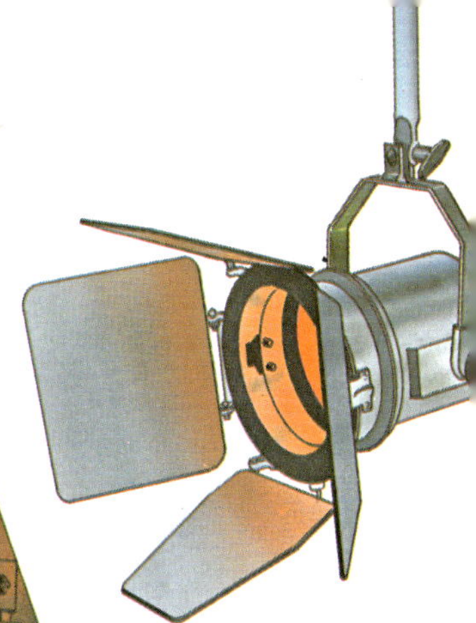

A lightweight lamp adjustable to 'spot' or 'flood' The metal flaps are known as 'barn doors' and alter the direction of the beam.

▲ Lighting is an important part of any programme and arranging it can take many hours.

The lighting director will use a variety of lights to achieve exactly the effect he wants.

Studio lights give off a surprising amount of heat, and a *lit* television studio is never cold!

On the floor

The producer and director are responsible for the planning of a programme and take final responsibility for it when it is transmitted. But they rely on highly skilled technicians, the studio 'crew', for the actual making of the programme. These are the people who work the cameras, the sound system, the lights. Each main section of the studio crew—cameras, sound, lighting—is made up of a small number of people who often stay together for months or even years, joining up with similar teams from other sections to work on a particular programme. Their schedule is dictated entirely by which programmes are to be made each day, and they can find themselves working on anything from comedies to current affairs.

Floor manager

The floor manager is the link between the director in the control room and the actors or presenters in the studio itself. It is his job to make sure that everybody is in the right place at the right time. One of his main tasks is cueing, letting the performers know when to start a scene or item, and how many minutes there are left. He hears the timings over his headphones and passes these on either out loud, just before the programme starts, or by special hand-signals when it is actually on (*see below*). If he spoke, of course, it would be heard in the programme!

Floor managers need to be good organizers, and able to keep cool under pressure. They also need tact, to be able to explain gently to an actor why the director wants him to repeat a scene for the fourth or fifth time. Floor managing is a responsible job, and is often a stepping-stone to a job as producer or director.

Camera

Studio. Cameramen in the studio are highly skilled technicians. They have to have a thorough knowledge of what a camera can achieve, for example what lenses to use in particular circumstances or what effect a particular filter will have. They also need the creative skill to choose exactly the angle from which to get a particular shot, or how close to the action to be.

Television companies usually have their own training schemes, but the people who join are expected to have some knowledge of cameras and photography. After an initial period, the trainee cameramen work on the studio floor, as assistants, helping to assemble the equipment and keeping the cables out of the way, before going on to become 'full' cameramen.

◀ The floor manager, having received instructions over his headphones, relays them to the actors.

▼ The signals used by the floor manager to relay instructions.

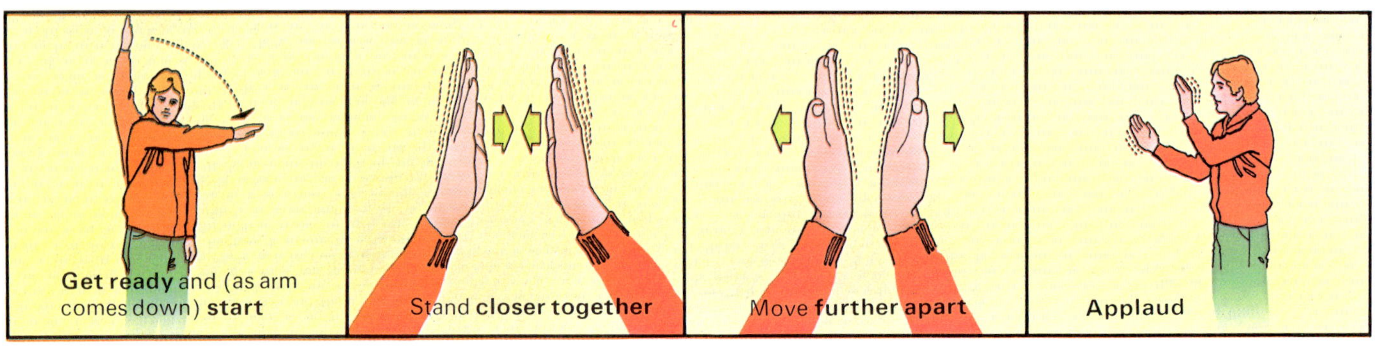

Film. Television also uses film cameramen (for a brief explanation of the difference between 'film' and 'studio' programmes, see page 29). A film crew is generally smaller than the studio crew: usually only 6 or 7 people in all, with only one cameraman and his assistant. The 16mm film cameras are smaller and lighter than studio cameras and have no cables, so they are more suitable for certain situations, like an interview in someone's home or for making programmes abroad.

Like snapshots, the film has to be processed, so there are no instant pictures as with studio cameras. This means that film cameramen carry a good deal of responsibility for getting exactly what the director wants. They often work long hours and can find themselves in tough situations: up the Amazon with a small group of tribesmen, or filming in the middle of a demonstration. This requires strong character and great adaptability. A good cameraman is very highly respected.

Sound

The sound supervisor is in charge of studio and control room sound. He plans the positions of the microphones before a programme and instructs the sound crew on the studio floor. They check the microphones, set them up in the studio and move them when necessary during a programme. In the sound control room, the supervisor balances and mixes the input from the studio microphones, adding special effects or sound from filmed or prerecorded sections of the programme. This takes technical knowledge and skill, and also the creative ability to choose the levels and effects most suited to each programme.

Television companies generally train sound technicians, though they are expected to know a certain amount about microphones, sound balancing and the principles of tape recording first. Starting as sound technicians on the floor, trainees can become boom operators and eventually sound supervisors, but this may take some time.

▲ A boom operator at work in the studio. The boom enables him to direct the microphone over the head of the actors.

Film. Sound recordists on films work on their own or with one assistant, and use a highly specialized tape recorder which they can sling over their shoulder. As with studio sound, they have a range of microphones to choose from, but they balance and mix the sound on their recorders as they go along.

Lighting

The lighting director is in charge of all the lighting arrangements in the studio, plotting the position of the lights for each programme. He works with an assistant, who operates the lights during a programme, and a team of electricians—'sparks' as they are nicknamed—who service the lights and make sure they are working properly. All lighting men are electricians, trained outside television. But television lighting requires particular knowledge of the way different lights look on camera and how to achieve specific effects, and this the 'sparks' learn through experience. Eventually, if they are lucky, they may become lighting directors.

Props

Every studio set contains a certain number of 'props', ranging from chairs to stuffed animals. All these items are in the charge of the property master, whose responsibility it is to ensure that everything a production needs is provided. He is also in charge of the props store, where all the items are kept. Here he has to look after props for a serial, for example, where a set has to look exactly the same from week to week: if a particular object is lost it might be very hard to find an identical one to replace it.

With him work a team of props men, who look after the props in the studio. There is no specific training for them. They usually join a television company as fit strong men able and willing to move very large pieces of furniture around, and may progress to property master after a few years.

Go-for

The call boy is the jack-of-all-trades, at the bottom of the studio hierarchy. His main task is to call performers when they are needed in the studio. But he often also ends up running errands, from collecting maps and charts from the graphics department to fetching sandwiches for the director's lunch. Being a call boy is really a way of getting into television, finding out how a studio works and then applying for other jobs—as trainee cameraman, floor manager or sound technician, for example—when the opportunity arises.

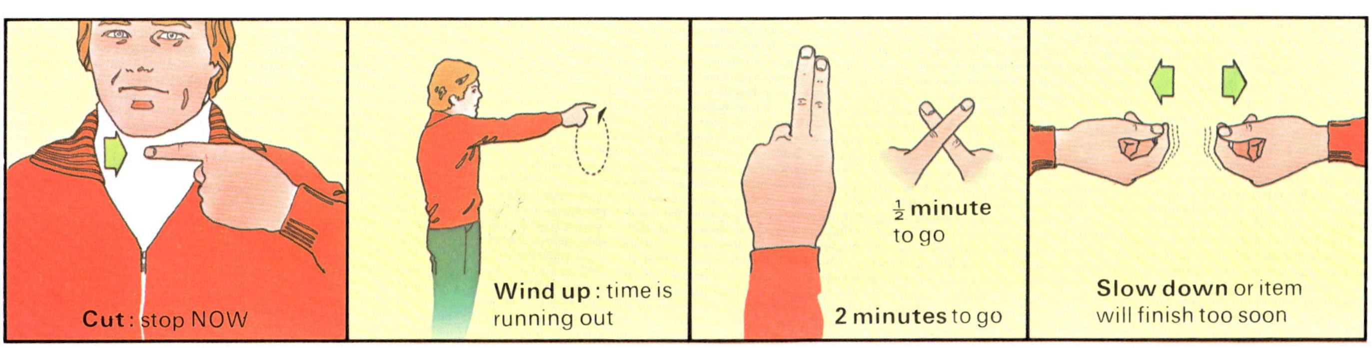

In the control room

In the production control room the lights are dimmed. Only the rows of monitors show up the faces of the people sitting tensely in front of them. The director leans forward, ready. On his left, the production assistant pushes a button on the desk in front of her: the 'ON AIR' sign lights up outside the studio, warning that no-one must enter now. She looks at the large clock on the wall and checks her stopwatch: '30 seconds to transmission . . . 29 . . . 28 . . .', she begins her countdown. The vision mixer on the director's right prepares to 'fade up' the first picture of the programme, from Camera One.

Behind a glass partition, in vision control, the lighting director and vision controller make their final picture checks. In sound control, the sound team prepare to play the opening music, the 'grams'. '3, 2, 1 . . .' 'Cue grams, take 1,' the director barks urgently. Immediately the programme's signature tune bursts out over the microphones. At the same time the vision mixer presses a button on his console and the monitor marked CAM 1 lights up with a red rim to show that that is the picture being transmitted now.

'Tighter on that close-up, please, 2.' At the director's words the picture on the monitor marked CAM 2 changes as the cameraman zooms in to a closer shot. 'Take 2,' says the director and the vision mixer responds instantly: the red rim around the monitor marked CAM 1 fades and springs up around CAM 2 instead. The director watches each camera monitor intently, checking every camera move. Around him, the technical supervisors check other monitors for picture quality, colour and brightness as the vision mixer switches expertly from one picture to the next, exactly as rehearsed.

The vision mixer has many of television's best tricks at his fingertips. With the one hundred or more buttons, levers and knobs in front of him, he can change the picture on any of the monitor screens. He can split the screen, to show more than one picture at once, he can change the colour of lettering on the screen, he can 'mix', 'fade' or 'dissolve' the picture on one screen into the picture on another. By means of a sort of electronic stencil, he can even change the shape of the picture. Today, the director wants the final shot of the programme encased in a bright red star. The vision mixer prepares that now on a spare monitor.

'One minute to end credits.' Suddenly the show is almost over. Tension begins to evaporate. Everyone sighs with relief: another programme has been successfully completed.

▲ In the control room the director watches the pictures from each camera on the monitor screens. On the console in front of him are the levers and buttons operated by the vision mixer.

◀ The lighting director controls the studio lights with the buttons on the console, while the vision controller checks picture quality.

▶ The director speaks brief instructions into the microphone. The production assistant calls the shots from the camera script. And the vision mixer switches from camera to camera.

The final touches

As we have seen, the selection of which picture to take from which camera in the studio is controlled by the vision mixer, instructed by the director. However, scenes for a programme are not always recorded in the order you see them on your screen. In a drama, for example, one actor may appear in three scenes spread over the whole play. It is easier to record all his scenes on the same day and shuffle them into the right order later. Sometimes different 'takes' of the same scene may be spliced together. An experiment in a science programme, for instance, may require several goes to get it right: the director may want to use the first part of one attempt and the second part of another. This will mean editing the videotape.

Videotape looks rather like sound tape, only it is wider and records sound and picture together. The simplest editing is done in the studio while the programme is being recorded. If something goes wrong in the middle of a scene, the tape is stopped and wound back to the moment *before* the problem occurred. The action is then repeated and recorded again, automatically wiping out the previous bad take.

If whole scenes need reshuffling, however, the editing will be done after the programme has been recorded. The newest system of videotape editing uses a computer. The director looks through the whole programme, scene by scene, and decides which shots he wants to keep and the order he wants them in. Then the videotape editor programmes the computer and all the shots he wants are automatically transferred to a second videotape, in exactly the right order. At this point the sound may need adjustment, or extra effects may be added. This is done in a special 'dubbing' suite, usually by the sound supervisor who worked on the programme in the studio.

Film editing is different because it is not electronic. Film is edited shot by shot rather than in complete sequences like videotape. On average, a director shoots about ten times as much film as he will eventually use in the programme. He views the processed film and then the editor actually cuts the film shot by shot and joins these together in the right order with special tape. This may take several weeks, because it needs great skill to choose the right point to end one shot and cut in the next one.

The editor and the director between them will probably recut sections of the film, or even the whole film, many times before the order and rhythm of it feel exactly right.

The difference between studio and film cameras

Studio. A television studio camera is electronic and produces 'instant' pictures. It works with a system of mirrors and lenses which distinguish—in colour cameras—three primary colours, red, blue and green, and reflects them on to three separate camera tubes. These are coated with a light-sensitive material which produces an electrical charge according to the amount of light falling on to it, and is then 'scanned' by an electron beam. This converts the electrical charge into an electrical signal, one for each tube. The three tube outputs combine to make a colour picture. These pictures can be transmitted 'live' or they can be recorded on to videotape, magnetic tape which records both picture and sound.

Film. A film camera uses light-sensitive film which has to be developed in the laboratory before any pictures can be seen. Television film cameras use 16mm film, which is midway between the narrower 8mm film used in home cine cameras and the 35mm film used for feature films. The film has to be joined patiently shot by shot and then sent back to the laboratory again to be processed for the finished programme.

▲ Film editing is a constant process of snipping and cutting individual shots, and the editor's room is always full of odds and ends of film. At the end most of them are thrown into the dustbin!

▲ The videotape engineer edits the programme after recording. He transfers it to a clean new videotape, leaving out mistakes and awkward pauses where necessary.

◀ This model of Moscow burning is only a few inches high, yet on screen will seem completely convincing. Special effects such as this are usually added at the editing stage.

▼ A rostrum, or fixed, camera, used for photographing stills such as old prints or paintings. These are then 'cut' into the programme where required during editing.

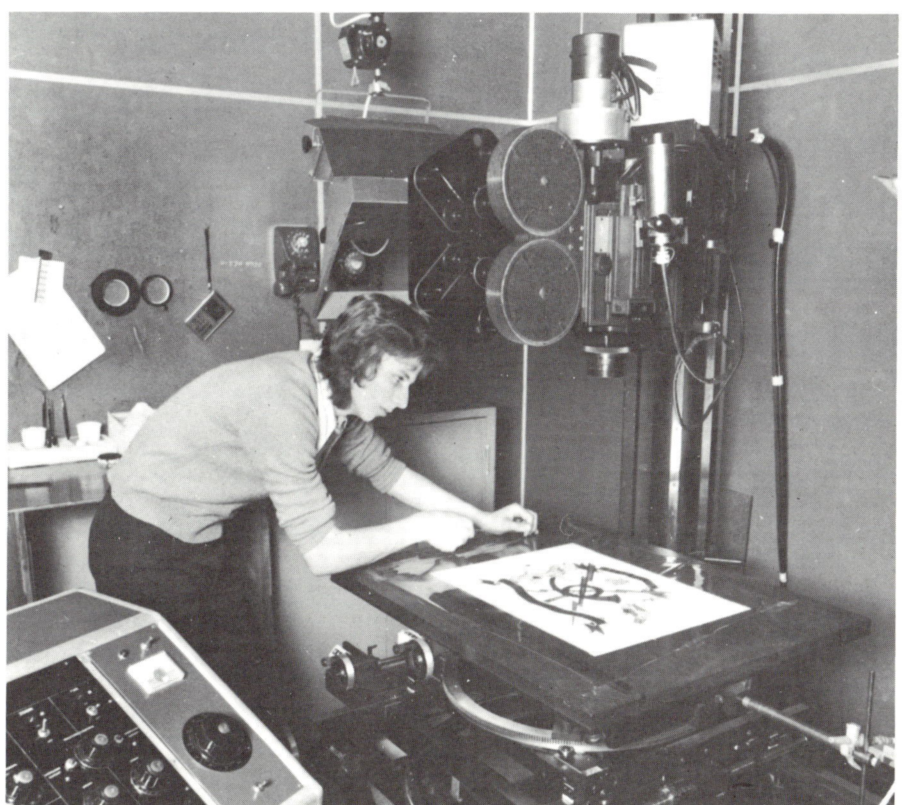

The editors

Making a television programme is rather like making a table. You start with an idea, or design, you prepare the pieces, then you assemble them and put them together. Editing is like putting the parts of the table together and adding the last coat of polish. It is the final process in the making of a television programme.

Vision mixer

All the pictures taken by the camera in the studio are joined together electronically by the vision mixer in the control room. Sometimes, in a play for example, the director gives the vision mixer a very precise script to work to, which tells him exactly when to change from the picture on one camera to the picture on another. At other times, in an interview programme, for instance, the vision mixer takes his cue from the director as the programme proceeds, cutting between cameras when one person stops speaking, or to see someone's reaction to what has been said.

Often the vision mixer has to cut very quickly from one shot to another or add a complicated effect. He may also have to add in, right on cue, filmed sequences, slides or parts of the programme that have been prerecorded. This takes quick thinking, quick fingers and much practice. All vision mixers are trained to operate the complicated vision mixing console, usually by the television companies. The entry requirements for vision mixers can vary enormously. A good education is important but vision mixers can have a variety of background experience, sometimes in the arts, sometimes the sciences.

▼ A videotape engineer. By pressing different buttons on this editing machine he can wipe out whole sequences, or adjust the order of scenes.

Videotape engineer

The videotape engineers are in charge of the videotape machines on which programmes are recorded. They have a two-way link to the studio control room and are cued by the director when to start the tape: the pictures from the studio cameras are then recorded directly on to the tape, rather than being sent to Transmission Control for immediate broadcasting as a 'live' programme.

If the programme is edited as it is being recorded a senior engineer will have to be prepared to stop and start the tape and wind it back and forward as required by the director. If the programme is edited later, he will help with the technical side of transferring the sequences the director wants to keep from one videotape machine to another in the right order.

Under him are a number of junior engineers, whose main job is to repair and maintain the machines, and who thus need a good working knowledge of electronics and engineering.

But the role of videotape engineers is slowly changing. New lightweight video cameras are making the use of videotape much more flexible and more popular for programmes where previously only film was considered suitable. These programmes often need shot-by-shot editing similar to film; as a result a new era of videotape editing is opening up where creative ability is as important as technical knowledge.

Film editor

When a film arrives back from the laboratories after developing, it is in the order in which it was shot, which is usually different from the final order intended. In addition, imagine a simple scene from a love story: an actor has to say 'I love you'. The director will have filmed him saying it from different angles, to get the best effect, and he will probably have done several 'takes' from each angle with the actor varying the way he says the lines to try to find the best version. So the editor will receive close-ups and wide shots of the same thing, sometimes with the actor smiling, sometimes with him looking serious. The same goes for other kinds of scene. Above all, there is always far too much of everything.

First, the editor views all the reels of film—the 'rushes'—with the director. Then his assistant sorts them into the right running order. Only then can the editor start putting whole scenes together. Between them, during the course of the editing, the director and editor will make many changes from their original plan before the film is ready.

▲ Synchronizing picture and sound. In film editing, where the pictures and sound are on separate reels, it is very important to make sure they are running exactly parallel. If an actor's speech does not coincide with the movement of his lips, the whole illusion of a programme can be spoilt.

Film editors need the patience to go over scenes again and again, changing the order of shots or cutting them in a slightly different place. Film editing is a mixture of technique and art. Experience can teach editors where to cut and how to piece a film together well. But very good editors also have a feel for the rhythm and pace of a film and this can make an enormous difference to the finished programme.

Most editors are trained in a television company and only become full editors after some years helping with the more routine work as assistant editors.

Sound mixing

Studio. Most of the sound on videotaped programmes is balanced and mixed in the control room while the programme is being made. But if a programme is edited afterwards, the sound between the edited scenes may be uneven and need re-balancing. These changes are done by the sound supervisor in the 'dubbing' suite. Here there is a large console containing all the sound equipment, and a television screen through which the videotape is played so that the sound can be matched to the picture. Music is often added at this stage too, or sound effects. Something like the slam of a door, for instance, must be in just the right place—it's no good after the door has closed!

Film. Film sound is recorded on magnetic tape, similar to that on an ordinary tape recorder, and the film editor actually cuts this and sticks it together at the same time as he cuts the film. But this can leave uneven sound between scenes. The sound has to be levelled out and extra effects added later, just as they would be on a studio programme.

There may be three or four separate sorts of sound—'tracks' as they are called—to mix together on even a simple film; more on a complicated one. This is done by the sound mixer in the film dubbing suite. He will not have recorded the original sound for the film and this is probably the first time he will have heard it. He works closely with the film editor who explains to him the kind of sound each scene requires and prepares a 'cue sheet', a chart with all the different sound tracks marked on it in colour showing exactly when one track is to be 'mixed' in and another 'faded' out.

The dubbing mixer has to make sure that all these sounds blend smoothly with each other and that they match the pictures. Getting this correct requires a lot of experience. Most dubbing mixers joined television companies as sound technicians and worked their way up (see page 25).

Cue for applause

Tonight an episode of a well-known comedy series is to be recorded. The director and actors have been rehearsing all week. The studio crew know what they have to do. An audience has been specially invited for the recording. Their laughter will be heard on the finished programme.

The studio looks rather more like a theatre now. There are rows of seats stretching far into the back. Then there is a 'moat' area where all the studio crew will work. At the moment that is empty. Beyond the moat, raised up, are the sets for the show, all ready and in position.

The audience file in, talking excitedly among themselves. They wrote off for tickets weeks ago. Now they are here, actually in the television studio, they can hardly believe their luck.

Suddenly a microphone crackles into action and a spotlight illuminates one man, standing alone in the 'moat'. 'Hallo, welcome to the show. I'm Donald, and I'm here to make you feel at home.' Donald is the warm-up man: his job is to tell the audience a few jokes so that they are in a good mood, and to explain what is going on.

'Above your heads, ladies and gentlemen, are small television monitors. On them, you will see the pictures the cameras are getting. You'll also see scenes that take place outside the studio which we have already filmed and which we'll be slotting into the programme as we go along.'

As he continues with his patter, the studio crew appear around him and pull their equipment into position. Then the lights dim over the audience. The actors walk in. A bank of very bright lights illuminates the set of a kitchen.

Suddenly two large red signs at each side of the studio start to flash: 'APPLAUSE'. The title appears on the monitors. At the same time, Donald claps vigorously and urges the audience to join in.

As the clapping gets louder, the floor manager cues the actors and the action begins. The first laugh goes up. The show is under way.

As each scene changes, the lights dim over one set and light up another. Actors and cameras switch nimbly between them. Then one of the actors forgets his lines and the whole scene has to start again.

Between it all, Donald pops up to help the audience watch the right set, or to amuse them when there is a hold-up. The audience rock with laughter. As the show ends they hardly need Donald and the 'APPLAUSE' signs to encourage them to clap. The cast take a bow. Up in the control room, the director and his team relax. The show is a success.

▲ The 'warm-up' man jokes with the audience to put them in a good mood.

◀ The studio audience sit in rows, rather like in a theatre, with monitors overhead to show how the programme is going.

▶ Variety shows are much easier for actors when they have an audience to 'play' to.

▲ The audience is urged to clap during the show by means of signboards displayed at appropriate moments.

On location

Obviously, it is not always possible to bring everything into the studio. Sometimes the 'studio' must travel to make an outside broadcast, known as an OB for short. All the equipment is loaded into special vans, one for sound, one for cameras, one for lights. One van, called the 'scanner', is specially converted into a small version of the studio control room. This is the centre of OB operations and is complete with monitors, a vision mixing console, and sound and light controls.

Today there is a typical OB: a horse race. The scanner and equipment vans drive to the location, which may be many miles away. They have allowed plenty of time: it takes several hours to unload the equipment, check it is working properly and get it set up in position.

The director has already chosen his camera positions: one on a special platform above the action, another at the finishing post, and a third mounted on top of a van to follow the horses round the track. He has also brought a 'creepie peepie', which is smaller and lighter than the other cameras. The cameraman will hold it on his shoulder to find unusual shots that the pedestal cameras could never reach.

As in the studio, all the crew wear headphones so that they are in constant touch with the team in the scanner. It is cold today so the crew are well wrapped up: they are used to spending long hours outside!

In a small room overlooking the track the commentator prepares for the race. He, too, has a two-way link to the director in the scanner, and a small monitor so that he can also watch the programme.

Filming takes place 'on location' too, but the film crew is much smaller than the OB unit. There is usually only one camera, which is much lighter than a videotape camera, and, because it is not electronic and has no cables, there is no need for a scanner or large equipment vans. The crew and their equipment generally travel together in one small van. Film is used mainly for documentaries, where videotape cameras would be too cumbersome and obtrusive.

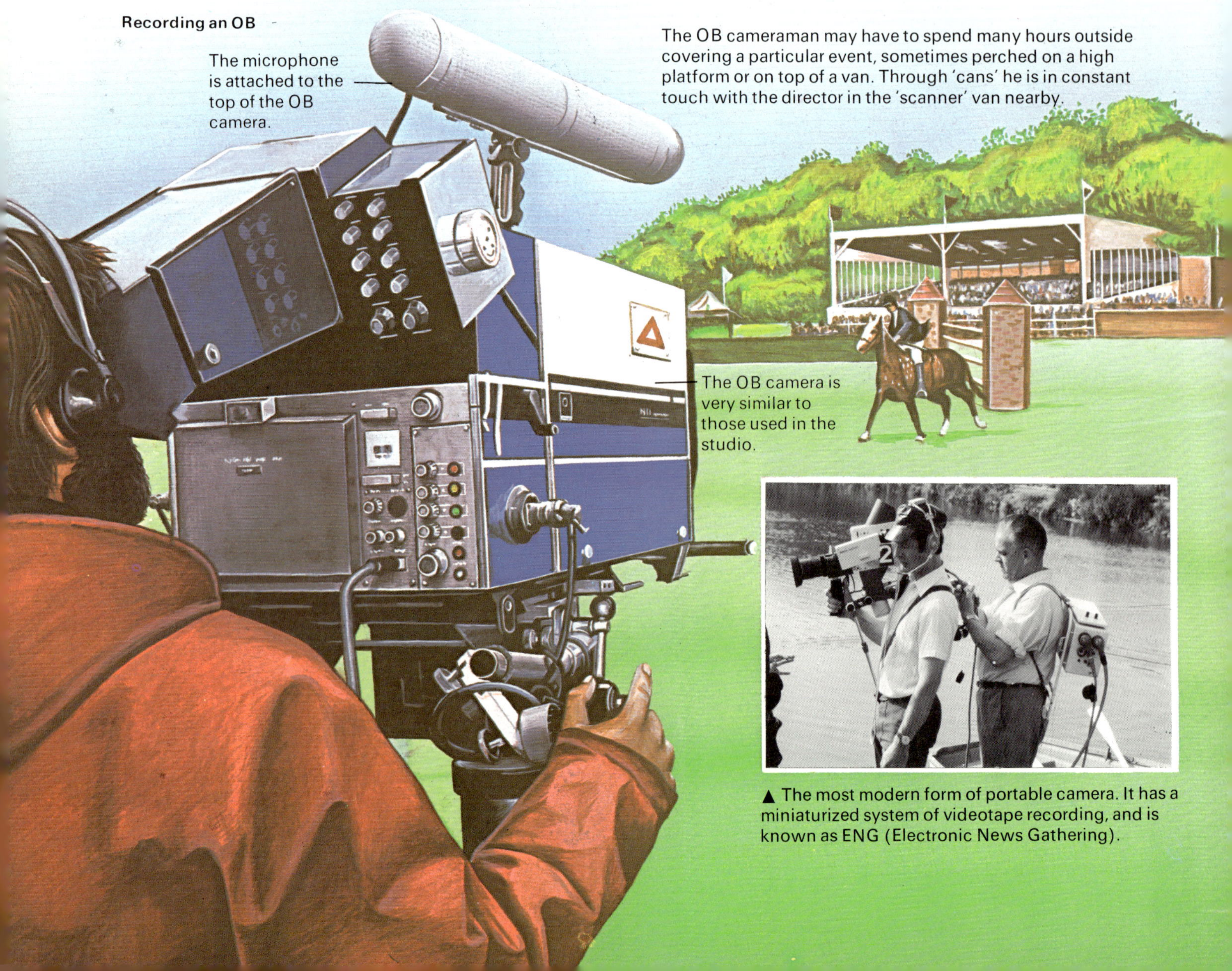

▲ The most modern form of portable camera. It has a miniaturized system of videotape recording, and is known as ENG (Electronic News Gathering).

▼ Filming a car journey. The car, with the actors in it, and the cameraman, are pulled along on a towing trailer, so that the cameraman gets a picture of the actors' faces with streets moving behind them.

▼ The film camera is smaller and lighter than an electronic (videotape) studio camera, and can be either hand-held or supported on a tripod stand, as in the picture. The 16 mm film is contained in the round 'magazine' on top of the camera.

A film camera

▼ With a film crew on location. Filming always involves a lot of standing around.

Bringing you the news

The average news bulletin has fewer words than the front page of many daily newspapers. Yet an enormous amount of time and energy goes into producing each news bulletin. Unlike other television programmes, news programmes cannot be planned weeks ahead.

Each day a team of chief editors, reporters and writers work together to assemble the news. Reporters are stationed all over the country and in key places abroad: they contact the news or foreign editors with interesting stories. Back home, the editors decide which of these stories to follow up.

News items are often on film. If this is coming from abroad, it is flown in by 'plane, rushed to the laboratories for processing, and then back to the newsroom for editing into shape. Or, sometimes, it is transmitted by satellite straight to the studio.

A team of writers prepare the news bulletins of the day, scripting each story or writing introductions for the films. By the late news there are a large number of stories to choose from. The producer of the day has to decide which ones are important and which ones to drop.

The newscasters come in and read through the script, adapting it to their own particular style. Often former newspaper journalists, they are the people we see on the screen. In case you were wondering, they do not have to learn the news by heart. There is a special machine, called a teleprompt, with a little screen which is attached to the front of the camera. The words of the script are rolled through the screen by remote control so that the newscasters can read them.

All news bulletins go out 'live', and the producer often has to make changes even during transmission. A piece of film may not arrive in time, or one story may run longer than expected and he has to decide to drop or shorten another instead. He tells the newscasters about this through their earpieces (discreetly tucked in one ear like a deaf aid) and they have to adapt accordingly while carrying on as if nothing had happened. Preparing and reading the news can be a very nerve-racking business!

Collecting the news
The pictures below show some typical events you might find in a television news bulletin. They have been collected by reporters all over the world. The reports arrive on the news editor's desk. Later the producer holds a meeting to decide which stories to include in the bulletin.

▲ The busy newsroom. Here the news editors and writers prepare the news bulletins.

▶ The teleprompt operator rolls a typed script through a special machine, at the newscaster's reading speed. A strong light shines on the words which are transferred by a system of angled mirrors to a small screen beneath the camera lens.

The newsreader sits at his desk. Behind him is a blue curtain. During transmission of the news, photos or film of the event are inserted on this blue background, by a process known as 'colour separation overlay' (or 'chroma-key'), so that they appear behind the newsreader, but not over him and he can still be clearly seen.

One day's viewing

Working out what programmes to show each day is very important. It is called scheduling. The person who makes the decision is generally one of the company's top executives, often known as the director of programmes. His job isn't an easy one.

He usually plans the schedule in 3-monthly sections. He draws up a giant chart, rather like a school timetable, which he divides into weeks, days, hours and quarter hours. Then he looks at a list of all the programmes he has available, with brief descriptions of what each one is about, and starts to fill them in.

Certain programmes always go out at fixed times—the news, for example, or a long-running serial. Those go in first. Certain hours of the day may be reserved for particular types of programmes—the afternoon for children's programmes; perhaps late night for adult-only films. He divides the programmes up into types to help him: comedy, drama, current affairs, children's, and so on. It is important to give the audience plenty of variety each day.

Sometimes he makes a mistake: a series may turn out to be less popular than expected but he has given it one of the best spots of the evening. So he may decide to move it, or perhaps to 'hammock' it, which means sandwiching it between two very popular programmes. The idea is that viewers will enjoy the first programme, look forward to the third, and so not bother to switch channels or turn off in between.

Most countries have more than one television channel and they often compete keenly for viewers. 'Ratings' charts are compiled showing how many viewers watched each programme. One of the arts of good scheduling is to keep the viewer watching your channel.

Some television companies also have commercials, and these have to be fitted around the programmes. This is where the presentation, or continuity, department take over. They are in charge of the detailed schedule for each day, checking exactly how long each programme runs, when the commercial breaks can be fitted in, and where to put announcements about future programmes. They have to make sure their timings are accurate to the last second because they usually have to co-ordinate with a 'network' of affiliated companies. They may, for example, be expecting to transmit a 'live' programme made by their own company at 17.05. If, as sometimes happens, the timing has changed slightly to 17.06 (because they have had to insert a station announcement, perhaps) they must let other companies know so that everyone can rearrange their schedules accordingly. Otherwise, they all will have one minute of blank screen—and a lot of puzzled viewers!

▲ Most television stations have an announcer, who appears on screen to introduce the programmes. The announcer's words have to be carefully planned to fit into the split-second timing of transmission, and he also has to be able to ad-lib at a moment's notice if anything goes wrong.

▲ The announcer's view of the rather small studio in which he sits. The camera, a fixed one, can be seen in the background.

▲ Television control rooms are dominated by digital clocks, keeping track of the time up to a 60th of a second. Split-second timing is crucially important both in the making of a programme, and in the transmission of it.

The evening schedule
This 'clock' represents one evening's typical viewing on television. The director of programmes has to make sure that there is enough variety, that the programmes shown at a particular time are suitable for the audience watching, and that, taken as a whole, the programmes fulfil television's aim, to inform, educate and entertain .

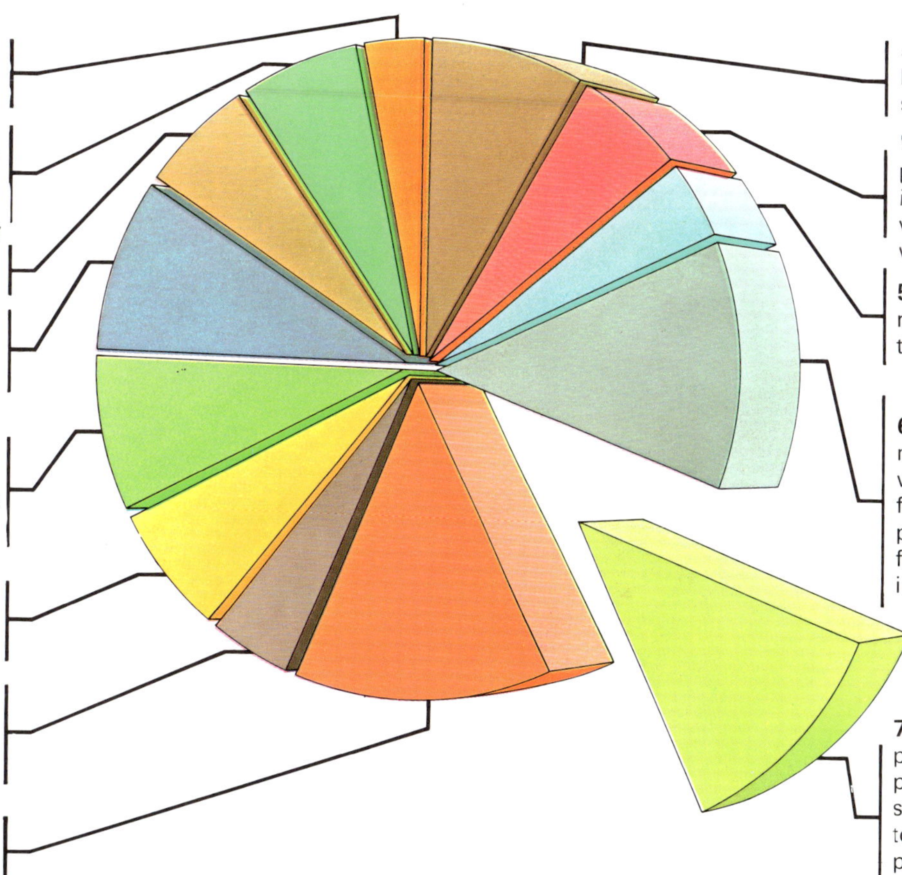

The back-up team

As well as technical and production staff, television companies have a management section which deals with the organization and administration of the company. This is headed by the company's chairman and the managing director, who between them make all the major policy decisions relating to the company. Under them is the Director of Programmes who makes the final decisions about what programmes the company should be making and, probably, looks after the scheduling (see page 38). But the day-to-day running of the company falls to a number of other managerial staff.

Programme controller

Programme controllers form the most direct link between the management and production sides of a television company. They are usually former directors or producers and therefore have a thorough knowledge of programme-making and a clear understanding of the problems involved.

Programme controllers are usually in charge of a particular department: light entertainment, features, current affairs, drama, children's or sport. They hire producers and directors, commission writers to work in their department and have overall control of all the programmes made in their department.

Sometimes the controllers think up ideas for programmes, in which case they are closely involved with the producers and directors in planning and preparing them. More often, they approve other people's ideas and then leave the producers fairly free to make the programmes as they think best. Obviously, however, controllers have different roles depending on which department they are heading. They usually have proven administrative ability as producers, and are always very experienced in their field.

Press and public relations

Every television company needs publicity to promote the company and let the public know what programmes are being made. Usually this is the responsibility of two allied departments:

The press office. Depending on the size of the company there may be several press officers assigned, like programme controllers, to the different programme departments. They spend a great deal of their time talking with newspaper journalists who specialize in reviewing television programmes, hoping to persuade them to say nice things about one of their company's programmes. This involves writing press 'handouts' about new programmes or series—anything from simple sheets of information to large glossy folders with photographs of scenes from the programme and information about the people involved.

They arrange to show the programmes at special 'viewings', to which all the journalists are invited, and often they give parties as well to launch a major new series, when actors and the production team will be there too, to meet the journalists and chat about the programme. There may be radio commercials to write and publicity posters to prepare, photographic sessions to arrange to provide newspapers with photos of the star. Press officers frequently have a background in journalism or advertising, as they need to be able to write well and fast, and to understand the needs of the journalists they deal with.

▲ A photo session arranged by the Press Office.

Public relations. The public relations staff promote the company's *image* rather than the specific programmes made there. Their job can cover a whole range of different things, from designing the colouring of the company's fleet of vans to arranging for stars of well-known television shows to open fêtes and make public appearances. They may deal with hundreds of requests a year asking for particular stars to appear at certain functions. They have to decide which offers are suitable and then persuade the stars to co-operate and make the necessary arrangements with their agents.

They are expected to come up with ideas too, like organizing open-days for schoolchildren to look round the studios, or planning exhibitions—of costumes from a popular historical programme, perhaps, or gadgetry from a science fiction series. They need to be able to mix easily with people and often join a television company after working in a public relations firm first.

Overseas sales department

The overseas sales department staff are responsible for selling the television company's programmes to other television stations abroad. They have to build up contacts with their counterparts in these companies, keep them regularly informed of what programmes they have for sale, and make all the necessary arrangements when a deal has been done.

To help with this, every year there are a number of television 'fairs' held around the world. Here, the sales departments from many different companies gather, meet each other and show off their programmes. Most of these programmes are recorded on special video cassettes, which are light and easy to carry abroad, even in quantity.

They are 'played back' on video cassette recorders, which are like ordinary tape

Selling a television programme

Television programmes are very expensive to make. Television companies try therefore to ensure that they are watched by as many people as possible. If the companies rely on commercials to make money, they can charge more for each slot if they can prove a programme is successful. The diagram here shows the three main ways in which a programme is sold, and some of the methods used in each case.

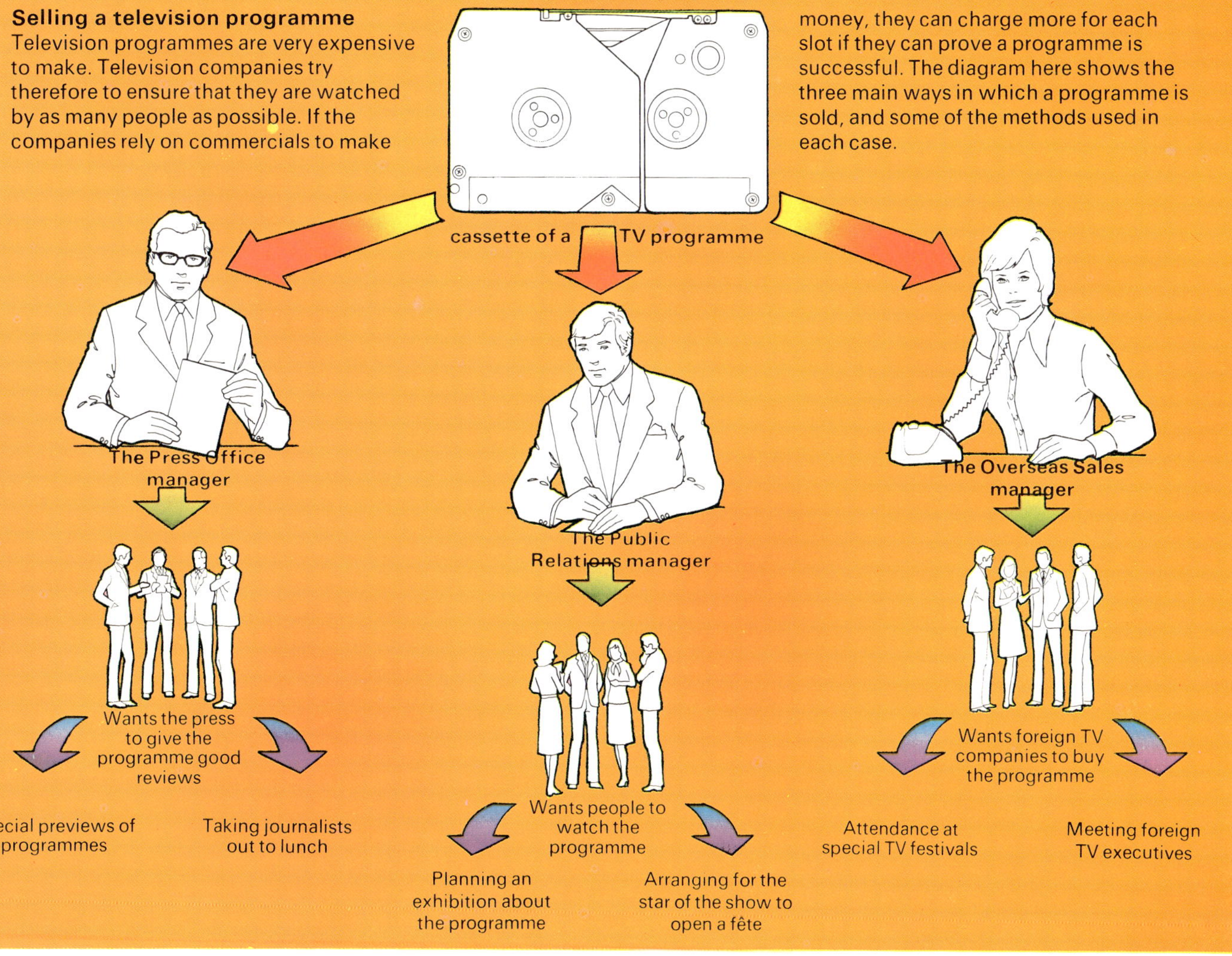

recorders but plug into television sets to show pictures as well. When a foreign company decides to buy a particular programme or series, they are then supplied with a copy of the original film or videotape suitable for transmission. It is up to the sales staff to make sure that these are shipped safely, arrive on time, and, if the other country wishes, are equipped with sub-titles or accompanied by a full translation of the script.

Most of the sales staff speak at least one foreign language. They also have to be good at organization, and the head of the team, who is often a senior executive, must have the ability to sell and promote his company's programmes abroad.

▲ Consulting the computer. In the complicated world of television, computers play an important role in providing information quickly and efficiently.

Head of presentation

Once the director of programmes has worked out the schedule of programmes for the next three months, with the date and time of each programme, he passes it to the presentation department. Here, the head of presentation rewrites it, keeping the programmes in exactly the same order but putting down the *exact* timing of each programme and inserting station announcements, local news broadcasts, weather reports, programme trailers and, if appropriate, commercial breaks. If his company is part of a 'network', he contacts the other presentation heads each day to co-ordinate his schedule with theirs. He has to be very thorough, good at detailed organization and will probably have considerable administrative experience.

The presentation department also organize the 'on-screen' trailers that appear between programmes.

Transmission controller

Once the head of presentation has rewritten the day's schedule, he gives it to the transmission controller who is responsible for the actual transmission of the programmes to the audience at home. He has to switch from one programme to the next and feed in announcements and commercial breaks at exactly the right moments, meticulously following the day's schedule. If something goes wrong—a piece of film breaks perhaps—he has to be ready immediately to put out an announcement or an apology. His job can be very complicated and requires split-second timing and quick thinking. Transmission controllers come to the job from a variety of backgrounds, and then train in the television company itself.

How the picture reaches your screen

One turn of a knob or press of a button and, as if by magic, a picture appears on your television screen. But you may never have stopped to think about how it got there.

Its journey begins in the studio where all the camera pictures are selected by the director and linked together by the vision mixer to make a programme. From there it is fed to a central control area at the television station. This is Master and Transmission Control, where the picture quality is checked and announcements and commercials are inserted.

Now the programme leaves the station where it was made as a series of electronic signals which are passed through cables to giant switching centres. There are usually several of them in each country, strategically placed in major cities. Their job is to receive the incoming programme from one television station and switch it across country, via transmitters, to another station, or direct to your home.

The television signals travel on two carrier 'waves'. The distance between the waves is known as the 'wavelength', and the number of waves sent out per second is the 'frequency'. Each television station has its own frequency, so that the viewer can tune in to whichever he wants to watch.

The transmitters radiate the programme signals to reach the aerial on top of your home, be fed into your television set and converted into the picture you see on your screen.

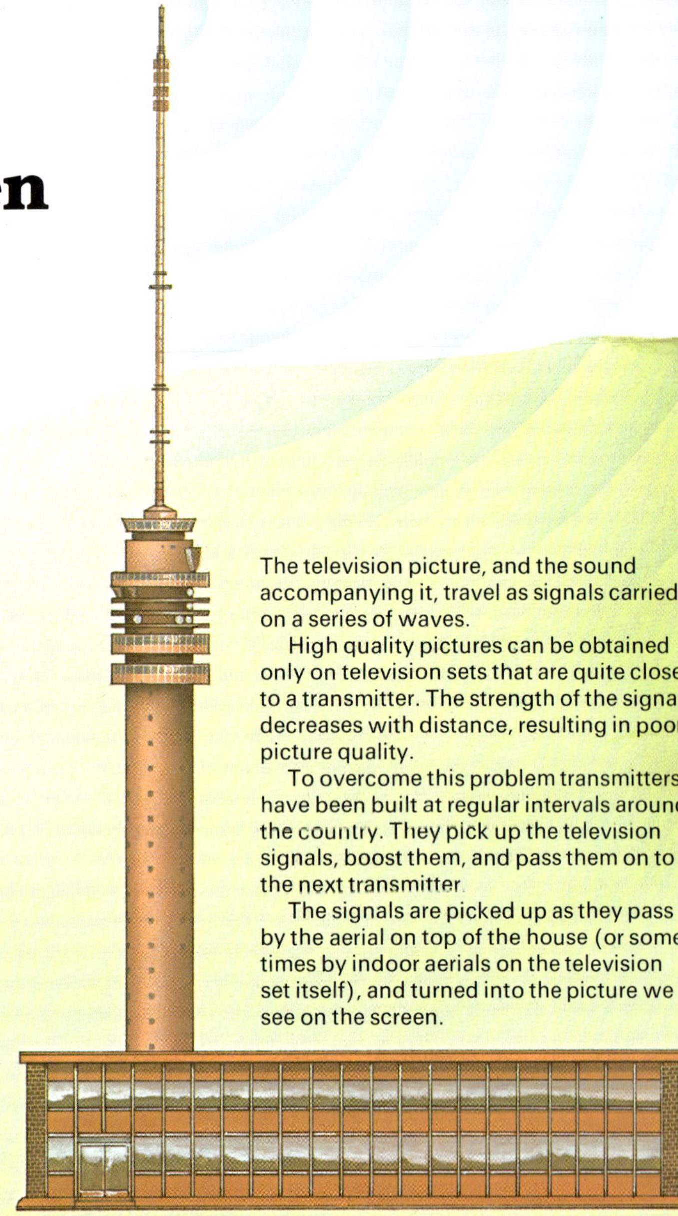

The television picture, and the sound accompanying it, travel as signals carried on a series of waves.

High quality pictures can be obtained only on television sets that are quite close to a transmitter. The strength of the signals decreases with distance, resulting in poor picture quality.

To overcome this problem transmitters have been built at regular intervals around the country. They pick up the television signals, boost them, and pass them on to the next transmitter.

The signals are picked up as they pass by the aerial on top of the house (or sometimes by indoor aerials on the television set itself), and turned into the picture we see on the screen.

◄ A programme being recorded in the studio. In due course the the picture will be fed into a central transmitting station (as above).

Television by satellite: communication satellites are used to send programmes from one country to another.

The signals are beamed from a special transmitter in one country to a satellite orbiting 32,000 km above the earth. The satellite transmits the signals back to receiving stations in other countries.

Reference section

General information

If you are thinking of a career in television, there is one important thing to remember: it is not easy to get into television, whatever job you choose. Television is a popular career choice and there is keen competition for a relatively limited number of jobs every year. This means that television companies can afford to be choosy, pick people with more than minimum qualifications, and expect dedication and very hard work.

Most of the jobs mentioned in this book require a certain amount of training, not necessarily in television itself. Television companies rarely recruit anyone under 18 years old and often recruit people after they have had experience outside television in a related field. So, although you may set your sights on a job in television *eventually*, it is well worth gaining experience elsewhere first. Areas to consider, depending of course on what type of television job you want, include audio-visual production companies, educational media, television equipment manufacturing companies, theater, still photography, or journalism. It is also worth joining clubs in your community, such as a photography, film, or theater group.

Employment opportunities
There are over 700 commercial television stations in the United States. The following three are the major national networks:

American Broadcasting Company
1330 Avenue of the Americas
New York, N.Y. 10019

Columbia Broadcasting Company
51 West 52 Street
New York, N.Y. 10019

National Broadcasting Company
30 Rockefeller Plaza
New York, N.Y. 10020

Most television stations broadcast network programs such as news and sports events, which would be too expensive to produce originally. Employees may number from about 30 for a small station up to about 250 for a large metropolitan area station.

There are also over 3500 cable television systems operating around the country and employing more than 25,000 people. Many additional workers are needed on a freelance basis: artists, writers, performers, musicians, and independent production staff members.

It is easier to gain initial experience in the television field in a small town before trying to compete for large station or major network positions.

Almost every state has public television stations (mostly educational) as well. They are often run by state or local agencies or colleges. A useful listing of educational TV stations can be found in a book entitled: *Your Career in TV and Radio*, while public TV stations are listed in *Your Future in Broadcasting.* A complete general listing of TV stations is given in a reference volume, *Television Factbook.* For details on these books see Booklist, p. 47.

Training and qualifications

Television is a high-pressure field and often requires long working hours. Dependability, enthusiasm, dedication, and the ability to get along with others are important attributes for anyone planning to enter the field.

You can begin to get a background for a television career in your high school by studying English, social studies, music and art appreciation. For technical jobs in TV, science, industrial arts, and photography are important.

Helping the audio-visual director or media specialist in your school can be an introduction to sound and visual media. Learning how to use and repair tape-recorders, cameras, film and slide projectors and to splice film is useful.

The various activities involved in student drama groups also provide valuable experience. Acting, building scenery, and doing lighting can give you a headstart toward TV work. Other areas to become involved in are writing for the school newspaper or playing musical instruments.

To enter the TV industry it is not absolutely necessary to have a college education. However, opportunities for advancement are much greater if you do. A combination of a liberal arts curriculum plus specific training in broadcasting or television and film production is desirable.

There are over 300 colleges which offer courses in film and television. Some of these are:

New York University
New York, N.Y.

Temple University
Philadelphia, Pa.

University of California
Los Angeles, Calif.

University of Alabama
University, Ala.

Indiana University
Bloomington, Ind.

A good listing of schools as well as a list of scholarships available can be found in *Your Career in TV and Radio* or in the current *Peterson's Annual Guide to Undergraduate Study* (see Booklist, p. 47).

Many television stations offer training in various areas in the form of internships either for college students or college graduates. Some broadcasting positions are controlled by unions. The requirements for attaining union status vary in different union branches throughout the country. One source of information on unions can be found in the book, *Getting Into Broadcast Journalism* (see Booklist, p. 47).

Further information on education and job opportunities in television can also be obtained from the following organizations:

Television Information Office
745 Fifth Avenue
New York, N.Y. 10022

American Women in Radio and Television, Inc.
663 Fifth Avenue
New York, N.Y. 10022

The National Academy of Television Arts and Sciences
110 W. 57 Street
New York, N.Y. 10019

Technical staff
To become a *camera operator* it is advisable to get training in photography and cinemaphotography. Knowledge of electronics is also helpful. A college background in broadcasting, mass communications, or television and film production would be advantageous for eventual career advancement. Further training is usually acquired on the job by being a camera assistant.

Sound technicians and *video persons* should have a background in math and science and some technical training in video production and editing.

Lighting technicians are all qualified electricians and need no specific television training. They learn the particular requirements of television on the job.

Film editors (for videotape editors *see* videotape engineers) are often trained after a junior post elsewhere in television or films.

Design staff
Set designers and graphic artists are usually recruited after completion of a relevant art school course. Set designers are expected to have a knowledge of history of art and architecture and training in technical drawing. Graphic artists need a knowledge of photography and typography. Yale University School of Drama, in New Haven, Conn., offers courses in set design, while many art schools and colleges, such as the School of Visual Arts, in New York, offer graphic arts instruction.

Sex discrimination
Every job in television can be done by either a man or a woman. In the past, certain jobs were almost always reserved for men, like that of cameraman, and others for women, like make-up artist. But now, fortunately, this is changing—and is, anyway, illegal. Although we have used either "he" or "she" instead of 'he or she' every time and terms such as "cameraman" to describe the jobs people do, this was purely to avoid clumsiness of expression, and does not mean the jobs could not be done by someone of either sex.

Costume designers are expected to have dressmaking ability plus art school training, including historical and modern costume design. Parsons School of Design, in New York, offers one good program in this field.

Make-up artists are often expected to have a diploma in hairdressing or

beauty culture and considerable practical experience in one or both. The television companies would then give specific training in television make-up. One school that offers a course in hairdressing is the Wilfred Academy in New York.

Production staff
Producers and directors are generally very experienced and have spent many years in television in other jobs. Direct entry training is very rare, even for graduates with a degree in some aspect of television production.

Researchers need no specific training and are usually recruited only after they have worked outside television, as journalists or teachers, for example. They are expected to have a well-rounded liberal arts education.

Floor managers are generally well educated and have usually worked backstage in the theater or as "gofors" (errand runners) in television before becoming assistant floor managers and learning from there.

Production assistants need good secretarial qualifications and experience. Television companies tend to give priority to secretaries already working with them when selecting people for training, so it is worth trying to join your local television company (the address will be in the telephone book).

Publicity and sales staff
Most of the people working in these areas have gained their experience in other organizations first. Press and public relations staff may be former journalists or from a public relations company, overseas sales staff may have worked for a foreign television company, for example. So if you are interested in this kind of job you should ask the television company of your choice what the requirements are and then set out to obtain the experience they suggest.

Useful words

Some useful words to know if you are thinking of working in television:

Action The moment at which action has to begin. The director often shouts "Action!" to mean "Start!"

Advance Person Person who makes a preliminary visit to a place to check its suitability for use in a program.

Boom A movable cart with a telescopic arm to which a microphone is attached.

Cans Headphones worn by the crew so that they can hear instructions from the control room.

CATV (Cable television) System of transmitting program signals by cables rather than over the air.

Chroma-key The method by which the color picture from one studio camera can be electronically inserted behind the color picture from another camera, thus providing a different background.

Credits The names of all the artists and production staff who have worked on a program.

Creepie Peepie A small hand-held television camera which is much lighter than an ordinary television camera.

Crew A general term for all the people involved in a production other than the actors.

Dubbing The process by which different sounds and sound effects are blended together once a program has been edited to give complete soundtrack.

Earpiece A tiny, wired speaker like a hearing aid, which a performer wears in his ear to enable him to hear instructions from the control room.

Flat A wooden frame with canvas or cardboard attached across it, used to make wall sections in a set.

Graphics The department which is responsible for designing and preparing all the lettering, captions and maps or charts that appear in the program.

Live The transmission of a program or event as it is taking place.

Monitor A high quality television receiver used in the studio or in technical control areas.

Network A group of affiliated regional television companies.

OB Outside broadcast. A television program made away from the studio with electronic cameras, not on film.

On location Literally "away from base" for the filming or videotaping of a program away from the studio.

PA Production assistant. Also the public address system in a studio.

Parallel camera A film camera, fixed in position over a table, which is used to take still photographs. These are sometimes edited together later to give the impression of movement.

Props Literally "properties": all the furnishings in a set.

Public television Non-commercial stations providing community services and educational programs and funded by the government, grants, and contributions.

Set The background scenery, or setting, for a program in the studio.

Shot The term used to describe each individual picture taken by a studio or film camera.

Take The term used to describe an attempt at recording or filming a complete sequence. Each take is numbered.

Telecine machine Equipment for projector enabling film or slides to be shown on television.

Teleprompter (trademark) A device which uses angled mirrors to project the words of a script onto a screen just below the lens of a television camera. This enables a newscaster to "read" a script without looking down.

Transmitter A tall mast with an antenna which is used to radiate television signals.

Videotape Magnetic tape on which a program made in the studio or an OB can be recorded.

Zoom lens A lens that can be adjusted automatically to give the effect of movement away from or towards the camera when the camera is, in fact, completely stationary.

Booklist

Anderson, Chuck. *The Electric Journalist: An Introduction to Video.* New York: Praeger, 1973.

Brown, Lester, *New York Times Encyclopedia of Television.* New York: Times Books, 1977.

Brown, Lester. *Television: The Business Behind the Box.* New York: Harcourt, 1971.

Fenten, D.X. *TV and Radio Careers.* New York: Franklin Watts, 1976.

Gordon, George N. and Irving Falk. *Your Career in TV and Radio.* New York: Julian Messner, 1966.

Hesener, K., ed. *Peterson's Annual Guide to Undergraduate Study.* Princeton: Peterson's Guides.

International Television Almanac. New York, Hollywood, London: Quigley Publishing Co., Inc.

Jackson, Gregory. *Getting Into Broadcast Journalism.* New York: Hawthorn, 1974.

Rider, John R. *Your Future in Broadcasting.* New York: Richard Rosen Press, 1971.

Shanks, Robert. *The Cool Fire: How to Make it in Television.* New York: Random House, 1976.

Television Factbook, Washington, D.C.: Television Digest, Inc.

Video Power: Grass Roots Television. (Young Readers Series). New York: Praeger, 1975.

Acknowledgments

Key to the position of illustrations: (T) top; (C) centre; (B) bottom; and combinations, for example: (TR) top right; (CL) centre left.

Artists
Adrian Day: 4-5, 19, 34, 35(T)
Temple Art Agency (Keith Robson): 6-7(B)
John Shackell: 9(TL), 14(CL), 25(CL), 30(BR), 33(BR), 40(TR)
Tony Payne: 13(BR), 14(B), 42-43
Terry Allen Designs: 20, 22(CR), 23(T)
Hayward Art Group: 24-25(B), 39(B), 41(T)
Michael McGuinness: 36-37(B)

Photographs
ZEFA: 9(BR)
BBC: 10(BL), 12(BR), 13(T) and (CL), 15(BR), 17(BR), 18(BL), 23(B), 28, 34(BR), 35(B), 45
BBC Design Group: 10(BR), 11(TL), 22(BL)
Thames Television: 11(B), 18(R), 40(B)
Yorkshire Television: 21(CR), 24(CL), 29(L)
TV Times: 21(BR)
John Neal: 29(BR)
Daisy Hayes: 44, 46
Shaun Skelly/Macdonald: jacket (front and back), 2, 4(TR), 6(TR), 7(TL) and (R), 8, 9(CB), 11(TR), 12(BL), 14, 15(CT), 16, 17(T) and (CL), 21(TL) and (TR), 22(BR), 25(C), 26(BL) and (BR), 27, 29(TR), 30(BL), 31, 32, 33(T) and (BR), 35(TL), 37(TL) and (TR), 38(TR) and (BR), 39(T), 41(B), 42(BL), 43(BR)

Information
The Author and Publishers would like to thank all those who helped in the preparation of this book: in particular the staff of Thames Television (and especially the Magpie team and the Thames training department), London Weekend Television, the Independent Broadcasting Authority, the BBC, and the BBC's Engineering Department.

Index

The numbers in **bold** refer to illustrations

1 2 3 4 5 6 7 8 9 Cad 84 83 82 81 80 79